Near Riviera Beach. Photo by Barrie Scardino. 1997

Cover: From the series **High Plains Farm**,
Adrian, Texas. © *Paula Chamlee, 1996*

Odessa 1936. Photo by Dorothea Lang, courtesy: Library of Congress

The myth that everything in Texas is bigger than life begins with the land, some 260,000 square miles of it, forming an olympian stage where big dreams meet up with hard scrabble realities. In popular images Texas is a state of contrasts: sprawling, scrubby plains spiked with oil derricks and populated by cattle driven along by wizened cowpokes, or clustered modern office towers where urban cowboys work a deal. To urbanized Texans, the contrast might be between city places and no place.

The reality is not so simple. In this issue of *Cite* we set out to explore the places in between — the vast rural landscape studded with small, sleepy towns, the edges, and the thin lines of transportation that sew it all together. This is territory where time moves sluggishly as the past gently collides with the future, and where hopes and aspirations and struggles to make a place (at a bigger, more abstract scale this becomes the stuff of allegories) are miniaturized in little dramas. The concept of the authentic, the original, may be disappearing from the landscape, rudely shoved aside and buried under so much universal, corporate newness. But it is not all gone. Maybe you just have to look a little harder to see it.

J.B. Jackson, the inveterate explorer of American places, described the landscape as "a rich and beautiful book . . . always open before us." It is a book that is continually being written, revised, and edited. As it evolves, the results are often distorted and in conflict, but the places that emerge from this struggle to reinvent the *genius loci* still remain the best evidence of how we learn to dwell. The myths about smaller and simpler places can be deceptive; as Colin Rowe and John Hejduk, who in their Texas Ranger days came to admire the clarity and order of the small courthouse towns in Texas, put it, "How much of the present susceptibility to these towns is merely nostalgic, how much is pure hallucination, and how much corresponds to reality is difficult to judge."

Bruce C. Webb and Nonya Grenader, guest editors

McMURTRY

A CONVERSATION WITH LARRY McMURTRY

In his novels, essays, and screen plays, Larry McMurtry has richly detailed regional cultures and vanishing ways of life in Texas and beyond. His epic novel of the old West, **Lonesome Dove***, won a Pulitzer Prize in 1986.*

Larry McMurtry was in Houston on April 19, 1997, to accept the Thomas Jefferson Award celebrating the inventive spirit from the American Institute of Architects, Houston Chapter. Mr. McMurtry met with Nonya Grenader and Bruce Webb, guest editors of this issue of **Cite***, and Drexel Turner to discuss Texas and Houston. Following are excerpts from that interview.*

Cite: Your collection of essays on Texas, *In a Narrow Grave*, was published in 1970. Many of them dealt with changing patterns in Texas. Perhaps you could comment on some of the observations from those essays, with the perspective that 27 years brings. We could begin with your preface: "Before I was out of high school, I realized I was witnessing a dying way of life, the rural, pastoral way of life."

McMurtry: I think the most obvious experience of my generation of Texans, up until that point in the 1950s, had been largely rural and small towns. Texas was still tied to some form of rural economy. Well, of course, the oil business was already strongly interspersed with an agrarian economy by then. Towns like Dallas and Houston began to boom right after the war, and they sucked people out of the small towns. The possibilities here and in Dallas, and to some extent San Antone, were just greater, so the kids began to leave the small towns and farms. My first three novels were written from a rural perspective. Then I wrote three that were set in Houston, showing the same migration from the other end — showing people who had been essentially country kids trying to become urbanites or at least suburbanites. That process has really been completed. A few people do go back after they've made whatever they make, but I think that the situation really hasn't changed very much. The vitality is in the cities, and there's not much of anything in the small towns.

Cite: What do they go back to do?
McMurtry: Well, they make their money in the cities, and they go back to do gentleman farming or ranching. Very, very few of the ranches left in Texas are working or profitable ranches. They're trophy ranches run by people who have made money and are still making it in other lines of work. The ranch cattle industry really isn't a viable business. It wasn't a viable business even then, in the 1970s. Most farsighted cattlemen saw that and prepared for it one way or another. So, now, when they leave the cities, it's just mostly for nostalgic reasons, I think.

Cite: You wrote, "What I didn't know then was that I was about to leave not merely the land itself, but also the rural point of view, in a sense the myth." Does the myth remain?
McMurtry: It's a pretty strong myth, and I think of most of my books as demythicizing. Particularly, I think of *Lonesome Dove* that way, but that's not the way it's read. It's read as a reinforcement of the myth. People don't see, or ignore, or don't want the critical aspects of that book, or my whole work for that matter. You could say that my whole work is essentially a critique of that myth — the myth of the cowboy. It will be understood by some people, but by the mass of readers, it isn't so perceived.

I was just reading a review last night of a book by Garry Wills about John Wayne and about some of the contradictions and, in relation to myth, some of the complications and paradoxes of the differences between the man John Wayne and the star John Wayne. The figure that he always plays represents a relation to this myth, and it's really complicated. The myth can be parodied, or it can be sliced up in various ways. But, so far, it has been indestructible.

I wrote a long essay some years ago in *The New Republic* that has not been refuted, about revisionist historians who see the winning of the West as a failure rather than as a success. It was a failure because of the destruction of the environment, the landscape, and the indigenous population. Businesses failed; whole towns, movements, migrations failed, leaving nothing but the land. This point of view began with Patricia Limrick and her study of ghost towns. Look at how many ghost towns there are, how they were founded with so much optimism; then look at how completely they failed.

My essay pointed out that most of the smartest people who lived through the winning of the West always saw it as a failure. They never saw it as triumphant. They always saw it as a harrowing experience that left many dead, and they weren't romantic about it. Some cowboys were very nostalgic, with a romance that continues to this day. But the most astute people of the 19th century who were involved in the process had some pretty stern things to say about it.

Cite: You observed: "There are places where the passage of the century apparently changes very little, and the Texas border is such a place." Is that still true?
McMurtry: It's true past a certain point upriver, but it's obviously not true of the Valley anymore. When you can fly big-time airplanes into the McAllen airport, which you couldn't do 15 years ago much less 35 years ago, you know it has changed enormously.

We just filmed two mini-series from *Streets of Laredo* and *Dead Man's Walk*. Both were filmed in the triad of Van Horn, Alpine, and Lajitas. Lajitas is still one of the most remote places in America. Cellular phones don't work there; it's fairly hard to get to, and it's hard to get trucks in there. If you want to you can go across the river in a little boat and eat Mexican food on the Mexican side. But all that stretch of river north from Del Rio is a huge smuggling area. You have to cross a lot of pretty barren country to get there. It's riddled with smugglers, and it hasn't changed a whole lot. There's a little bit of a tourist industry, but that's about the only thing that's changed.

You know, my stories should be set in the Panhandle of Texas or eastern New Mexico. They shouldn't be set down on the border. But the area between Fort Davis and the border — Alpine, Van Horn, and Lajitas — is the only place you can go and turn a camera 360 degrees and not see a telephone pole or any evidence of the 20th century. We looked all over the state. There are a few places left, I'm sure, in the High Plains where you can do it, but they're too far away or unfeasible.

Another 20 years will take care of Marfa, and that whole area. Alpine is already spreading over towards Fort

Davis, and Marfa is going to be a considerable complex of communities based entirely on tourism. Already you can see little subdivisions leaking out from Van Horn toward El Paso, and vice versa. It will always be spacious country, but it's not going to be what it is right now, and it's not going to be what it was at the beginning of the century either.

Cite: You said that the East Texans are molded by the South and West Texans by the West. How?
McMurtry: Well, I perceive maybe five cultural areas within Texas. I was just over in East Texas for a college basketball tournament. It's always been the South. The South is contiguous from a little bit east of Dallas, say Greenville, all the way to the Atlantic coast, as far as I'm concerned. There's not a huge difference in attitude between people in Tyler and Longview and people who live in Mississippi and Georgia. It's pretty much the same culture. I am often irritated because I'm thought to be a Southern writer, but I'm not a Southern writer at all. The part of Texas that I'm from is Midwestern. North central Texas, from Fort Worth up and pretty much over to Amarillo and Lubbock, is very Midwestern. It's not any different from Kansas.

Cite: Dallas has always impressed me as Midwestern. Is it like Kansas?
McMurtry: Dallas is a little bit of a hybrid, but the country around Dallas is very Midwestern and the attitudes of the people are very Midwestern. Houston is less of a Southern city than it was when I came here in 1954. The boom has moved it culturally farther west, in an L.A.-like direction. Then you have Hispanic Texas along the border and in San Antonio, and then the mountain states Texas, west of the Pecos. All those are pretty different cultures to me — South, Midwest, Houston (West Coast), mountain states, and the border.

Cite: Is San Antonio still one of your favorite cities?
McMurtry: No, it's never been one of my favorite cities. I'm critical of San Antone. I don't know it as it is today. I never go there. San Antonio was a lovely old city; now it's a lovely city to visit, but it's a very closed, old-money, tight city.

What I've always liked about Houston, and this distinguishes Houston from Dallas, is its openness, its welcomeness. Anybody can get along in Houston with a little energy and a little likability.

This is not true in San Antonio. There, they are very glad to see you come and visit, but they don't really know what to do with you if you live there. I know that San Antonio is growing. I imagine it's gotten a little less that way because it's a much larger city than it was when I wrote the *Narrow Grave* essays. It was a kind of small city, a miniature Denver in a way.

Cite: You make these keen observations about things changing from what they were, then changing again and again. I get the feeling that you feel very sad about that. Do you think we could have done it differently, or is it just the way things happened? I don't know if it's a critical stand.
McMurtry: No, it isn't. I feel that the settling process of the West was pretty inevitable. There was the pressure of people that wanted land. I don't see that much could have changed the way it happened.

I think that, in me, I've seen and felt a clash between the values of the frontier and more civilizing values. I have a ranch house that still sits on the very place that my grandparents homesteaded when it was still frontier. There were five settler families in Archer County. Most of that strip of counties in central Texas, south of Wichita Falls and north of Bandera, was settled very late because of the Comanches. It's only been settled 110 years. So it's possible in one lifetime (mine) to have known my grandparents who came here on a wagon from Missouri in the 1870s and took part in this settling process and raised children that continued the settling process — children that went to the cities and studied. In the first two generations, of course, it was about surviving. It was about staying there and making a living and nailing down a foothold on what really was a frontier, but it wasn't a savage frontier by that time. I've just finished the last of the *Lonesome Dove* series, called *Comanche Moon*. It's about the breaking of the power of the Comanches, the end of the Comanche wars, and the 1850s, 1860s, and 1870s.

My grandparents basically waited 100 miles east of where they finally settled because the Comanche area was too scary and too violent. They probably wouldn't have survived because it wasn't safe. They came with a real frontier attitude and ethic, which their children — there were 12 of them — worked out of, but only a little bit. They recognized the

value of education. I think at first they saw it as a practical value more than anything else. I was born in the Depression, and I have a little bit of a memory of what the Depression was like and a lot of memory of how the Depression scarred people in that region and all over the country. But I knew right away that I wanted to leave the land for the things of the city, particularly the education and literature.

So, if I'm sad about the older generation, it's only because I was close to them, close enough to my uncles and aunts and grandparents to see how whatever creativity and imaginative capacity they might have had was given no chance to flower because of the hardness of the struggle to survive.

Cite: If you look at the changes that took place in the last 30 or 40 years, there is a sadness in your work about the loss of something and some question about what we've got now. You say, for example, "San Antonio was a lovely old place."
McMurtry: Now, it's not. But I don't feel that way about Houston. I've never liked Dallas. I've never seen any hope for Dallas. It's larger and richer, but it's no different culturally than it has always been. The only reason that San Antonio has changed is because it's sucked in so many new people that the old oligarchy can't really control it as they did for a long time. Houston really has never been controlled, not in my time, not since 1954. It's always been fairly wide open, filled with graft and corruption, but it's dynamic and energetic. And I don't have any regrets about the development of Houston. It has a lot more nice buildings now than it did.

Cite: But what about the changes in rural America — how we've traded small-town life for the suburbs?
McMurtry: I think that life in the small town is really more barren than life in the suburbs. At least you have video stores in the suburbs, and you can buy a book here and there. On the other hand, up to a point in life, I think you can profit from just the strength of the country, the strength of the landscape, and the beauty of the landscape. But I think that point is during your teenage years. I'm glad I grew up in the country. I'd be a little bit farther ahead in some respects if I'd grown up in the city and had city possibilities at a younger age, as my grandson is doing now in Austin. But I also got a focus and a sense of locatedness from

growing up in the country that set me in good stead. It's a mixture — there are good things about both.

Cite: As for change in Houston, does it surprise you that the Astrodome is now basically obsolete?
McMurtry: It does in a sense. But I haven't kept up, so I pronounce about Texas cities cautiously. I've had four different periods in my life in which I've had some contact with Houston. I first came as a student in 1954; I left and came back at the end of the 1950s as a graduate student; I left and came back again in the mid 1960s as a professor; finally, I left for a long time and came back in the 1980s as a bookseller with my little shop over in the Heights. And I can't say that the vibes of the city have changed very much over all these years. Always, one of the attractions of Houston is its funkiness. There seem to be a lot of overlooked parts of Houston that only people who live here know about or ever think about. But I don't have a sense of Houston having become something I wouldn't like. I always like to come here. I don't like to go to Dallas, and I don't like to go to San Antonio. I don't like to go to Austin either.

Cite: When we wrote you, asking about a favorite Texas place, you replied, "I expect Rice is one of my favorite Texas places." Could you elaborate?
McMurtry: Well, Rice is one of the nicest campuses in the nation. What I like about it is that it's in the center of a really dynamic city, and yet it doesn't dominate the city, nor is it dominated by the city. For example, the University of Texas dominates Austin, and the University of Wisconsin dominates Madison. I don't like a university that can dominate a city, but do like a university that can sort of hold a dignified place in the center of a huge city; I still feel very attracted. I was just over there, and I feel very serene at Rice. I think it is an excellent environment in which to get a good education.

Cite: What attracted you to Rice?
McMurtry: You know, it was the purest of accidents that I went to Rice. My father wanted me to be a vet, and I seemed destined to go to A&M. I didn't much want to, but I had no clear sense of what I wanted to do. But I knew I didn't want to be a cowboy or a cattleman; I knew that very early. And I was passing through the living room, and the television was on. I think that we had just got-

ten the television set; I don't think we had had it a week. I saw a program about Rice that said it was tuition free, and that interested me. I didn't really know what Rice was. It was an institute then, I did know that. So I called and came down here, and I liked the looks of it. I almost didn't get in because I came from a tiny little high school. But I got on the waiting list, and got in at the last minute in August the year I was to enter, which was 1954.

It was sort of ironic. I don't think I could have gotten in even a year later. I had no math, so I was completely lost. I saw that it was hopeless my sophomore year, and I went to North Texas State and graduated from there. I came back to Rice and got an M.A. here when I didn't have to worry about math. I've had a long involvement with Rice. I'm coming back to do the President's Lecture in September in a place I just barely got into and could never have graduated from with a B.A. Yet it still draws me.

Cite: So, you have a great story for an introduction to your President's Lecture.
McMurtry: I do, don't I? I do.

Cite: The course of things did change in the mid 1960s?
McMurtry: Yes, and I was here in Houston when they changed. I was a Rice professor here from 1963 until 1971, although, during the last two years, I was on leave doing some things. Rice itself changed. They saw they had no future as a scientific institute, and when they leveled out the humanities and the sciences, it worked fine. I think it's a much better school now; it's certainly less constricted and less narrow than it was when I first came. On the other hand, I came to Rice in time to have contact with some professors who were here when the school opened, professors like Will Dowden and Alan McKillop who came out of a very solid and substantial academic tradition.

Cite: Is Washington a place that appeals to you as a city? Many people don't seem to set much store by Washington as a place to live.
McMurtry: Well, it's kind of accidental with me. I might have stayed at Rice my whole life, but it didn't turn out that way. I got a chance to go into the rare book business and open a book shop in Washington, which I still have. It's been there 27 years, and I'm going there tomorrow. To me that was a lot better

balance with writing fiction than teaching. It's very different; it takes a completely different kind of energy. It's very relaxing to me. I'm still building a book town up in Archer City now. There are eight or nine towns in the world that are essentially built around books. And that's what I'm doing to my town. I have four buildings, three of them full with 400,000 books. There are no viable businesses in town. It's too close to Wichita Falls. I'm going to turn Archer City into an international book town. I've just begun to advertise, and there are people coming all the time from all sorts of places.

Cite: We were lucky enough to have gone there just a few months ago. It was phenomenal — the space itself with the barrel vault, places to sit and read, and the area with the Texas books — it's really wonderful.
McMurtry: It's going to be a very nice place. It's about two or three years and 200,000 or 300,000 books from being quite what it needs to be. It still needs a lot of shaping. Actually, I have enough books because it's kind of a dying business. I'm being offered a lot of book shops. I've been buying book stocks of businesses and book shops that are going out of business; I've already bought about 20 or 22. So it's kind of an anthology of American book shops as they once were. It's very exciting to me. It's what I really want to do now — build my book town.

Cite: Why aren't you building it in a city? There's not even a motel nearby.
McMurtry: I'll tell you exactly why. Because second-hand books do not generate the kind of money that you need to pay urban rents. That's why all the bookstores in America are dying. There used to be a million bookstores and secondhand bookstores in all the cities of the East and Midwest and West Coast. There's only one of those gigantic bookstores left — in Portland, Oregon — because urban real estate is worth too much. So I went to a town, Archer City, where the buildings cost $30,000 to $40,000 apiece, and I can have a million books with almost no overhead. But there's no big city where you can do that. The family in Portland has had its own house for, I guess, 75 or 80 years. They've owned their whole block for a long, long time.

Cite: Your books are so lovingly dis-

played. When I commented on the vast collection, a person standing next to me said, "Well, have you been across the street?"
McMurtry: We have three buildings full, and we are going into another very, very large building. That will probably do it. The other building will hold as much as we've got already — about 700,000 or 800,000 books. And that's enough because it will replenish itself in a sort of tributary fashion by then.

Cite: When you're in Archer City, do you use the bookstore as a resource?
McMurtry: When I'm there, I work in it. I have only three people working there, and when we get 30,000 to 40,000 books at a time, which is what we've been buying, it's a huge job. All these books need to be priced and arranged. I try to buy stock from shops because the books are already priced. Even though some of them aren't priced correctly, at least there's some price in the book. We have so many books that we aren't worried that somebody is going to find a $10,000 book for a dollar or something like that. If somebody goes in and finds it, they can buy it. They will find some sleepers because I simply don't have time to look at every book myself, and I simply can't hire enough people to live and work there. Only book people would want that kind of job. But that's okay. That's part of the fun of it. I figure I'm about 40,000 books behind in pricing — that is, 40,000 books with no price in them at all. They've been bought from private libraries, and I haven't gotten around to them. I hired someone for the summer to come in and price for three months. It's not hard; it's just that somebody has to take every book off of the shelf and put a number in it.

Cite: It's interesting to think that you could build a town with a bookstore as its industrial base. If you had that and a hotel and a restaurant . . .
McMurtry: Well, there's already one bed and breakfast, and I'm sure there will be others. There is a restaurant that goes in and out of business. I don't own it or have any interest in it, but it does occasionally open up. I think eventually there will be enough dealer traffic from buyers to support a couple of restaurants and a coffee shop, maybe a couple of beds and breakfasts too. It's going to come.

Cite: You have said, "The cattle range had become the oil patch." So, what's next?

McMurtry: Well again, the oil patch is what there is until you get to the cities, and then you get the oil patch plus the computer patch. But oil is still going to be the only viable industry out in my part of Texas because there's nothing else. There are still people who farm, and, I guess, some who make a living at it. But not many people ranch and make a living at that, unless there's some other form of income, or they have oil.

I don't know what comes after the oil patch. Maybe working for a living just goes on and on. It seems to. It was already the oil patch when I was growing up there. The first oil boom in that county was in 1918. That's a while ago — 80 years. When it falls off that's accepted. A lot of my customers at the book shop (and I have customers from all over the world) come to Archer County to invest in oil wells and oil leases. And they see these bookstores, and they stop and are amazed. A lot of them are from New York, California, Chicago, somewhere like that. We don't really depend on foot traffic that much; we depend on dealers. But I have noticed that among our best customers are oil people from far away.

Cite: You commented on your fondness for Rice, and we were curious about other places in Texas that remain wonderful for you, not just in your memory.
McMurtry: Well, you know, there aren't that many. I like Houston. It's the only Texas city I like. I don't mind some of the others but I have no attachment to them. I have a genuine attachment to Houston. I've written four books and two movies set in it. I think it's a wonderful, interesting, diverse, great city, but I don't have any feeling for other Texas cities. After Houston, my feeling would be for Rome or New York City. And I have some feeling for Los Angeles. I have a toehold there; I've had an apartment in L.A. for a long time. I don't at the moment have it, but I go back and forth. I've worked in and around Los Angeles for 40 years. I do go back; I basically like the place.

Cite: Deyan Sudjic wrote a book that was read by a lot of people in architecture and architecture schools called *The 100-Mile City.* He wrote a lot about Houston and Los Angeles. One of his points was that cities were becoming these great, dispersed, amorphic things. He said that Houston seemed to him to be about 20 years behind Los Angeles but moving in the same direction. Do you agree?
McMurtry: I know the writer, but I don't

know his book. But the comparison between Houston and Los Angeles is obvious. They have almost the same surface area. At the time I wrote that *New Republic* essay, they were about 650 square miles apiece. Neither one had a proper center; they had a number of centers. I still feel that way.

You know, when I go to L.A., it reminds me of Houston; Houston reminds me of it — the freeways, the cars, the new architecture. But the natural landscape of Los Angeles, its natural site, is a bit more interesting. It's not a flat coastal swamp or plain. I've lived in the San Fernando Valley, and I've lived in Santa Monica. I never spend continuous time in Los Angeles. I'm there two weeks — that's about as long as I've ever stayed there in the 40 years I've worked in films out there. I think it's an interesting city.

Cite: In the essay "A Look at the Lost Frontier," you drove from Brownsville up through Texas. Have you done that lately?
McMurtry: Well, I haven't done it again in a literal sense. Even that trip was mostly invented, although I did mostly do the drive. But I still made up almost everything in it.

Cite: How did you work your way through *Lonesome Dove*? Did you do a scouting trip?
McMurtry: No, I've never done anything like that deliberately. But I've been all over the West many times, speaking and traveling. It's never been intentional — driving up that way to look at the trail where the cowboys went — but I have been to all those places, so I pretty well know what it looks like.

Cite: Were you in Houston when NASA arrived in the 1960s?
McMurtry: Yes, I was here when NASA arrived. I was a young parent then, raising a child more or less by myself. I was aware of the astronauts; I met them a few times, but I never went out there.

Cite: I wondered about the impact that had on the city's sense of itself — like the baseball team used to be the Colt 45s, then came the Astrodome and the Astros. Houston is constantly reinventing itself without looking back.
McMurtry: Well, that had started when I wrote about the Astrodome, but I didn't really see much of that progression because I was in Washington for the next 15 years.

Cite: When you come here, do you go back to old haunts like Spanish Village or places like that?
McMurtry: No, I really don't. I come here to buy books or to make a speech. A goddaughter of mine and her boyfriend are both at Rice, so I come and visit them for parents' day or something like that. I always have a reason for coming here. Unfortunately, I'm rarely here for more than a day. Like I got here at noon today, and I leave at 6:30 in the morning. I had lunch over on Westheimer. I don't seek out old haunts. Most of the people I knew best — not counting a couple of academic people at Rice who are very much alive and very good friends — are dead, or very, very old and not visitable any more.

Cite: Are you generally happy with the locations used for your movies set in Houston?
McMurtry: I thought that *Terms of Endearment* was a very good movie. I wasn't particularly thrilled by the use of Houston. And I don't remember much about Houston in *The Evening Star.* When you think of a movie about Houston you think it's going to be like Robert Altman's *Brewster McCloud,* which I thought was very good at getting the sense of Houston.

I was just by one of the houses that were used in *Terms of Endearment* this morning, and it's not what you think. It's not what you notice about those films. You don't say, "Gee, this is what Houston is like!" You say, "Gee, this is what these people are like!" It doesn't really use the city in a spectacular way.

I've written two tetralogies — the Houston tetralogy and the *Lonesome Dove* tetralogy. You know they're written catch as catch can, not in sequence or with any real thought. I have a lot more confidence in the Houston books working than I do in the *Lonesome Dove* tetralogy, in which I try never to mention how old a character is or how far it is from one place to the other.

Someone sooner or later is going to do an index or companion to the *Lonesome Dove* volumes to identify the places that are mentioned and try to figure out the ages and names of the characters and things like that. I am very careless about those things. I write very fast, and I never have the right reference book when I need it. I write about a street, and then I forget about it, so I'm sure that, like any serial novels, there are a lot of inconsistencies.

But the locations probably do work in the Houston books because those four books are all set in one city, like *The Alexandria Quartet,* for example. That is a lot easier than writing four books in which your characters are scattered from 100 miles below the Mexican border to the Canadian border. I shudder to think that if I tried to look at the *Lonesome Dove* books, how many inconsistencies and impossibilities geographically I would find, not to mention the ages of the characters and stuff like that. But Houston is easier; I'm pretty close on Houston.

Cite: There is a colorful cross section of Houston places in your books, like McCarty Drive.
McMurtry: Oh, yes. I wonder if that place is still over there. It used to be a great old honky-tonk, a crumbling sort of Spanish honky-tonk.

Cite: Right, it looked like a bird dog.
McMurtry: About two years ago, I got over to the Athens Bar. That's the last time I was over that way.

Cite: To close the interview, you have said, "Prose, I believe, must accord with the land. . . . A viny, tangled prose would never do for a place so open; a place, to use Ross Calvin's phrase, where the sky determines so much."
McMurtry: Yes, Ross Calvin and the story of New Mexico. Yes, I think that's right, and Houston is tricky because it's not the plains. Most of my prose is a plains prose because I really am a creature of the plains. This is a coastal plain, but I've always seen it as an urban forest, so I don't know how my prose works out in relation to Houston. I'm pretty confident of it, though, in relation to the plains. ∎

Booked Up, Archer City. Photo by Nonya Grenader, 1997

"I'm still building a book town up in
Archer City now. There are eight or nine towns
in the world that are essentially built around books.
And that's what I'm doing to my town."

Graves Ranch "Hard Scrabble," Glen Rose.   Photo by Bill Wittliff

"For a writer like myself, the place has been a source

of fascinating material."

OUR OWN PIECE OF COUNTRY

John Graves

As a native of Fort Worth, I can't lay claim to a rural childhood and youth. But my family, like many in the 1920s and 1930s, had links to rustic ways through farmers and cattlemen and small-town merchants and lawyers and such folk in its background, so that our home tended to assume that country things mattered, that you needed to know about them. Within trudging distance of where I grew up, there was unspoiled land along the Trinity River's West Fork — preserved against development by the long stasis of the Great Depression — where I and a number of friends like me used to camp and hunt and fish and learn a little about wild creatures and the places where they lived. Later, in the summers, I worked for a country relative at plowing and wheat harvesting and fence building, and from the start there were also long visits in Cuero, far to the south, where my father's people had lived for what seemed like forever, at least in Texas terms, and where cattle and crops, the bases of the region's economy, were always absorbing topics.

All of that lodged itself in me, though it went dormant during the years that followed, years of college and war and New York and Mexico and Madrid and a number of varied elsewheres. But it awoke again strongly in the late 1950s after I came back home to Texas for an intended brief visit that has somehow lasted until now. And before long, the rural virus led me into buying a hard-used, pretty, secluded patch of cedar-covered limestone hills in Somervell County some 50-odd miles southwest of Fort Worth, where in ensuing decades I chan-neled much energy and what money I could muster into building a house and outbuildings and fences and roads, and into clearing brush so that little creekside fields could be sowed to forage crops and elsewhere range grasses could take over from the ubiquitous cedar. The aim was to turn the land into a working stock farm and a good place for our family to live, and within a few years this more or less came to pass.

The stock farm as such was never a smashing financial success, nor had I expected it to be. The sale of calves from the 25 or 30 mother cows that such a rough and rocky tract would nourish dependably, after the enormous soil loss caused by overgrazing and cotton farm-ing in the late 19th and early 20th centuries, did not lead to riches. Still less income derived from goats, of which we had plenty at times because they happily eat and control resprouted brush, though they're vulnerable to predators that happily eat goats. By and large, though, the animals paid their way and a bit more, provided entertainment and drama large and small, and at certain times of the year required work in the form of birthing and doctoring and castrating and sorting and such, work that viewed objectively was probably worth more than the beasts themselves but which we mainly enjoyed because it was . . . well, pleasant, if you were built to appreciate such things.

So was other work with a garden, a vineyard, bees, an orchard, and construc-tion. And so too was the place itself, with clear White Bluff Creek that flowed well most of the time; the teeming wildlife; the broad vistas from high places; the hillside secret crannies that children could discover for themselves afoot or on horseback; and the succession of good dogs we had over the years. Our daughters — both of them married city-dwellers now — remember their life here with pleasure and gratitude, as do we aging elders. The land has helped to shape our family and shape it well, which mitigates the fact that in modern econom-ic terms our use of it has been pretty much of a bust.

Economics is a fluid study, though. For a writer like myself, the place has been a source of fascinating material, and by utilizing it as subject matter in print, I attained nothing resembling wealth but a fairly adequate living for a span of years. So maybe that's where economic justifica-tion for the whole arduous and satisfying enterprise can be found, if indeed such justification is needed.

~~~

The region itself, the expanse of rough hills of which most of our small county is a part, has been badly abraded by history. Its sloping soils were washed away swift-ly during hard early use for grazing and farming, and as living grew skimpier, large segments of the population hauled out, moving on west or to cities. By the 1920s the scattering of hard-bitten yeomen who remained had evolved a minimal economy with two main cash products. One of these was cedar fence posts chopped from the brakes that had taken over the ravaged land, and the other was illicit whiskey brewed and distilled in secret niches among the brushy hills.

Glen Rose, the county's seat and its only real community then and still, enjoyed a degree of profit from its repu-tation as a spa, based on some fine stinky artesian wells whose sulfurous flow was said to have therapeutic virtue when bathed in or imbibed. But a good share of the imbibing done by patrons of the local sanitariums, operated by "rubbing doctors," seems to have involved not sul-fur water but moonshine spirits smuggled down from the hills in jugs and Mason jars. Glen Rose had a wide reputation as a center for the distribution of this beverage during Prohibition and for decades afterward, since much of West Texas stayed legally Dry into the 1960s and remained an eager market. The tough Anglo-Celtic natives who made the stuff were much harassed by the law, which led to many fine tales of pursuits and escapes and conflicts and occas-ional killings.

A majority of locals, however, eschewed such drama and continued to farm what flat soil still existed on the little tracts they owned or tenanted, ran a few gaunt cattle and hogs, and chopped cedar posts, which at crossroads stores were sometimes a medium of exchange for flour and snuff and shoes and other exotic needs. For sport they often ran hounds at night after coon and fox and bobcat.

In that special little world, which I first glimpsed in the late 1940s when I started going to the area to hunt and fish, a sort of undemoralized poverty remain-ed the norm even after wartime and post-war booms had rejuvenated cities not far away and had sucked away more hill people. The stubborn survivors liked it where they were, despite agricultural and pastoral devastation. They knew from experience that they could subsist on this land and, more importantly, they *belonged*, hanging onto dignity and wholeness. They knew the hills' private wrinkles, and who had what quirks of character and who lived where in valleys drained by clear running streams, and ancestral shades stood beside them as they labored for small return. When I bought the first part of my own place in 1960, locals would still work hard at building fences or digging foundations or any other task you needed done, for a fat two dollars a day.

In a world like ours, all this was bound to change. When key West Texas cities like Lubbock went Wet, the moonshine trade collapsed. Migrant cedar choppers, often Hispanic, took over most of that activity, and, for that matter, steel posts forged in distant mills, more durable and easier to install, were coming into wide use. Decent urban wages, abetted by a new war in Vietnam, kept on tolling natives elsewhere. And increasingly people from the cities, like me, had begun to buy land in the region, very cheaply at first. Many of us intruders could only afford one or two of the old homestead tracts into which most of the land was divided, but others had the wherewithal to combine many such tracts into good-sized ranches bulldozed clear of cedar, dotted with small lakes behind earthen dams, and fenced tightly with net wire to contain herds of Angora goats, whose mohair brought in a tidy profit, while the goats themselves controlled new brush and fitted in well with the cattle that grazed new grass. By and large, these activities were good for the country itself, but they displaced old human ways.

An appetite for change also began to emerge among the area's natives, especially those in little Glen Rose, whose envy was aroused by the boomish growth of other towns nearby. Granbury in particular, the seat of Hood County, just north of Somervell, waked up from a long rustic doze to find itself burgeoning from the construction of a big reservoir on the Brazos River with thick residential development along its shores, as well as from the town's bedroom proximity to Fort Worth. Confronted with such humming prosperity only a few miles away, Glen Rose boosters wondered when, if ever, they would get their shot.

They found out in the early 1970s, when construction of a nuclear power plant was begun in the county on a Brazos tributary called Squaw Creek, which was dammed to provide cooling water. There was not much opposition to the project in the county itself, where increasingly change of any sort was being viewed as good. But environmentalists in the Dallas–Fort Worth complex kicked up so much fuss and maintained such a critical glare at the details of construction that the plant didn't go on line until 1990, by which time its cost, originally estimated at $779 million, had swelled to about $12 billion. Undoubtedly all of this made us county residents much safer than we might otherwise have been, and these days the thing sits there with its twin reactor towers perking along, and pays taxes of millions on millions of dollars into the county's coffers. There is good fishing in its lake, even in winter near the warm-water outlet.

Myself, I'd just as soon not live about six miles from such an installation if given the choice, but I wasn't, and for that matter a number of decades of life in this century have turned me into a sort of pessimistic accepter of most changes. One change harder to adapt to than the nuke itself, though, was the disruption of local life caused by its construction. At one point, some 11,000 persons were employed on the project, a fair proportion of them natives of the region, but the rest migrant skilled and unskilled workers from all over the nation's map. Many found places to live in neighboring communities such as Stephenville, Granbury, and Cleburne, but plenty settled nearer to the job, often staying on after the job was done. In 1970, before the uproar started, Somervell County had a censused population of 2,793, a figure not much different from those registered every decade for the past 40 or 50 years. By 1980 it held 4,154 people, and in 1990 there were 5,360, of whom a small minority were the old tough hill people I had come to understand and like.

In thus entering the modern world and acquiring wealth, the town and county have undergone many other changes either good or bad, depending on one's viewpoint. Newcomers keep arriving, some to buy pretty land at high prices, others to retire in predominantly Anglo surroundings, or to open small businesses, which mainly flourish if well conceived, or ("carpetbaggers," an uncharitable native friend of mine calls these) to see if by some stratagem they can cause a bit of that copious tax money to trickle in their direction.

The local schools are now housed in large solid buildings surrounded by athletic facilities, a far cry from what used to be. The hospital is a state-of-the-art structure, well equipped and staffed. A highly regarded new golf course spreads beside Squaw Creek, miles downstream from the nuke. In the hills above the course, an amphitheater regularly presents a musical religious pageant called *The Promise* to large and appreciative audiences during the warm months, while not far away, shelter for stock shows, ropings and other equestrian competitions, weddings, country music concerts, and similar public events is provided by a big exposition center.

Et cetera. All new, or at any rate quite recent.

~~~

And us Graveses, here in our enclave on White Bluff Creek? What has the advent of modernity meant to us; what disruptive changes have we had to face?

In honesty, most changes thus far have been of our own devising, except for the sad loss of our live oaks to the wilt disease, a misfortune we share with thousands of other Texas landowners. The place still sits at the end of a small county road that stops at our gate, and the country on other sides is still sparsely peopled hills and pastureland. With the departure years ago of our main source of auxiliary labor — the daughters — Jane's and my interest in going ahead full steam with such time-eating activities as winemaking and beekeeping and vegetable gardening gradually waned and at last evaporated. And finally, in the late 1980s, with age invading my joints and stamina, I somehow ceased to derive great pleasure from patching fences and getting kicked by cows in chutes and sold the little herd, our goats having gone to market a couple of years before. The only cattle using the place now are batches of steers brought in during the growing season by a younger friend, who tends them and keeps the fences tight.

The land itself is being reblanketed by cedar, and I watch the invasion with equanimity. So be it, something within me says; we have "done that." For all this has been not so much a defeat as a slacking off, and life here is still good, if much less strenuous. The house, 25 years or so a-building, is finished now, and though it is much too big for the two of us, on long weekends when friends and children and grandchildren come, it fills

up and resounds. Birds and wild beasts surround us as they always have. The creek still flows well much of the time, if not as copiously as it used to (depletion of the aquifer below by multitudinous new wells seems to be the main reason), and I can usually go down with a fly rod and catch supper from it when the notion strikes. Sunrise and sunset are peaceful patches of glory, and if I spend a great deal more time now in reading and contemplation than in wielding hammer and saw and fencing tools, I guess it was time for such a shift.

Threats loom, of course, for we have not been granted timelessness in an era ruled by change. The chief such menace for a couple of decades now has been the possibility of a reservoir on the little Paluxy River, into which our creek flows below the place, a project dear to the hearts of many local boosters. Rationales both for and against it are complex, and I won't delve into them here, but those of us who live in the river's valley and love it and believe that Glen Rose can find its water elsewhere have put up a pretty good fight, a successful one so far.

So yes, change threatens even here. But when and where, these days, does it not? ∎

Graves Ranch. Photo by Bill Wittliff

Booker Hole, Graves Ranch. Photo by Bill Wittliff

ON LEAVING TEXAS

Rosellen Brown

It's high summer and, even in Houston's most emphatic season, I am saying a reluctant good-bye to Texas after 15 years. Now that I am living a few blocks from the lake that gives Chicago its extraordinary physical uniqueness, I am reminded daily of one of the two charms I missed in Houston — mountains and water (the bayous hardly count). A University of Houston architecture student once illustrated a beguiling little book of Houston stories with photos of the city behind which he'd inked in a scrim of fictional mountains. ¡Mira! El Paso with skyscrapers!

One does learn to live without all but man-made beauty in Houston, to say, "That RepublicBank Building is real nice." Some days are lovely enough, some neighborhoods and vistas extremely pleasant. But, to be honest, in all my years there, every time I returned from a trip to a city more handsomely endowed by nature, I came home angry and had to wait until my life recaptured my attention, till the feel and look of my days became again relatively, not absolutely, tolerable.

But my not-so-brief sojourn in Texas has left fond indelible marks in my memory, and this seems a good moment for a valedictory recounting of what I've found striking there.

Close to home, the least dramatic, but the place whose loss gives me the deepest pain, is my neighborhood. My Saturday morning ritual included a long spell of sitting on the cement-and-brick steps of my little wooden bungalow, one of the gray-and-white Menil cottages with their vernacular "everyman" feel, that face the ascetic Rothko Chapel and the unadorned façades of the University of St. Thomas dormitories. The light that filtered through our large magnolia and pecan trees was perfectly softened; the temperature of the long comfortable season was ideal until late in May, when the smarmy season begins. A lovely informal peace prevailed around the loosely controlled space of the Menil "compound" — neatly cropped grass and park, home to countless happy dogs; the authority (moral as well as visual) of the Barnett Newman *Broken Obelisk* that stands over the chapel's dark-bottomed reflecting pool; and the relative silence of the university /museum block. The neighborhood is perfectly scaled; both private and public in feel, architecturally sub-unpretentious, casually but not carelessly tended: with all its oxymoronic implications, a lively oasis.

I spent many an hour there, surrounded by my cats, facing out, because neither the peace of my fenced yard, the dead

calm of the suburbs, nor the intrusive urban buzz of the inner city can provide the interest of a street where many pass, but quietly, not in crowds, where something might happen — a wedding party breaking out through the doors of the Rothko (in latter years the scene of too many AIDS-related funerals); a passing friend out for a stroll; a busload of eager tourists looking down from their great height. Though it is hardly the most opulent, the corner at Branard and Yupon is the one I always considered the most favored in Houston.

My perambulations around the state were not thorough or particularly unusual, but I have twice written under challenge for the *New York Times*'s "Sophisticated Traveler" about places my provincial Eastern editor attempted to convince me did not exist. One is the Port of Houston. ("But Houston isn't a port!") That port was the culmination of an almost secret mosey in a canoe down Buffalo Bayou from way west in Katy, through burgeoning woods, amid birds and fishes, right under the roaring 610 Loop, so near and yet so far from Neiman's, between the only naturally steep banks in town, all the way into the city (a trip now interrupted by the stepped waterfalls in the back yard of the Wortham Center), and on to the rusty

hulls of the big ships and industrial realities of the Turning Basin. All this is part of the unglamorous, not-for-sale Houston unseen by the casually dismissive eyes of convention-goers and passers-through-the-airport-and-the-Galleria, like that New York editor.

The other watery domain, so close that it's nearly commutable, is the Big Thicket, unknown to a surprisingly large number of Houstonians. A peculiarly fragmented set of habitats east of the lyrically named Old and Lost rivers, the Thicket, with its deep darkness and fecundity, is an instructive discovery to anyone whose stereotyped vision of Texas makes the whole state desert and cottonwoods. Of all its many parts (separated now by the insensitive surgeries of commerce), for me the most memorable was a boggy meadow of pitcher plants, stretching their slender, pink-veined, carnivorous throats to the sky, literally as far as I could see. In general the entire area, beginning around the Brownwood subdivision in Baytown and the submerged communities nearby, long since abandoned to encroaching waters, has left my imagination piqued. Panthers crying in the forest, strangling ropy ty-ty vines looped tree to tree, waxy flesh-colored cypress knees poking out of a swamp — this is the Texas of seep and flood, not dust and sunlit fire, furtive, lonely, haunting. It is hard not to believe the stories of ghostly presences alive and hidden among the trees there. Beaumont photographer Keith Carter's enthralling book of photographs, *The Blue Man*, honors the mysterious place and its inhabitants, and, yes, the feeling that it's overseen by invisible, intangible witnesses.

Big Bend, of course, deserves to be its own state, if not its own country. To this day, maybe ten years since my single visit, I cannot see a full moon without recalling the Christmas when we sat bathed in white light in the nearly intolerable heat of the hot springs at midnight, our hands diddling over the side of the brick enclosure that was once the foundation of a health resort building (ten cents a day, we heard) into the icy Rio Grande. We leaped into our nightclothes to keep the warmth in and drove hell-bent back to our campsite and into our sleeping bags. Damn fools we were, too, camping out in December. A few weeks later we read that a couple of hikers perished out there in a sudden snowstorm.

~~~

I am notorious in my family for being a light-seeker. I suspect I'm an undiagnosed SAD (seasonal affective disorder) sufferer. In any event, I rarely work at a desk because I'm doomed to follow illumination around the house, setting myself down before the brightest window as the light changes overhead. So Texas is a series of light and dark spots for me: open highway, all sky, too stark in summer to be stared into; the endless beach at Mustang Island, where everything is white — gulls, sand, horizon; the butterfly museum in Houston, rain forest in a silo, sunny and damp, glowing vegetation and tilted delicate wings; my daily dappled walk up and down the live oak corridors of North and South boulevards, light/shade, light/shade in stripes and polka dots on the cobbled paths.

My memories of Rice are of a beautiful deserted campus, like a lovely face

kept too sheltered for character lines. The University of Houston I remember as a serviceable, unintrusive habitat dutifully planted and tended, unobjectionable and uninspired, epitome of the word "pleasant." This is not a matter of class; no one, after all, would call the University of Texas campus inspired.

I have a sense of the desultoriness of Montrose, of old thick red lilies, graceless, worn around the edges; wood rotting in the subtropical dampness; so much ramshackle deterioration east of Montrose, and so many valiant homeowners gussying up their houses with Victorian doors and effortful gardens north of Alabama. The drive to Intercontinental Airport on Highway 59, with its dilapidated houses and homemade commerce (palm readers, Pentecostal churches, shaky little businesses), was in such contrast to the endlessly unscrolling name-brand clones making Interstate 45 so depressing that I stayed off it on the way to the airport except under duress.

Houston is where I first saw good restaurants in concrete shopping malls; a house with a huge plastic mustang rearing on its lawn; and neighborhoods with drycleaners on every block. Whole plazas, where every store feels like a trivial luxury, provide parking that is ugly and ubiquitous and free, which has made me unfit for Chicago, where I must now commit what feels like my entire salary to unburden myself of my car just to eat a meal or see a movie. Texas is where I saw my first heart-stopping sunsets, and blankets of blue and orange and yellow along the highways in spring. Those bluebonnets of Lady Bird Johnson's are arguably the most important contribution of any First Lady since Eleanor Roosevelt.

Houston is where a concrete-sided bayou runs stinking alongside all those streets that begin with Braes. Though I'm not sure I believe it, I've been told that Brae is not fake Scottish but somebody's name — Bray. Houston is where Glenwood Cemetery makes a park of genuine and serious beauty, right in the

shadow of the skyscrapers and the far less elegant plots of Sixth Ward. Houston is where my heart seizes up when I drive around the otherwise undistinguished corner of Richmond and Buffalo Speedway near the Summit, where the Rockets gave me supreme moments of joy when I hadn't realized I could care so much about a ball and a hoop — partly, perhaps, because the thrust of the big city was there with us, CLUTCH CITY signs in our car windows. I devoutly hope the Rockets don't abandon the Summit, which is a comfortable and modest building with terrific sightlines.

Trade-offs: I wish a greater variety of heat-hardy flowers could survive in Texas gardens. I never got over my suspicion that more people ought to try, at least, to nurture a less conservative horticultural mix. I wish there were decent radio stations in Houston. Talk-free KUHF is nothing less than a scandal compared to nearly every station in the NPR network. But there are marvelous cafeterias.

How does one compare? I wish there were more solid old houses, and I'm hardly the first to dream of a live downtown accessible by decent public transportation. Nonetheless, Houston is the most convenient huge city in the nation. This is not just a matter of space and speed of movement: when a repairman says he'll be there, he shows up on time. Unless you're stuck on a freeway, Houston gets out of your way. Possibly, if it had a more aggressively interesting profile, it would be more intrusive. New York and Chicago pay for their texture: they do get in your way.

When we drove north toward Chicago, Texas held us nearly half the way. Buildings along the highway border were humble, low-rent, wood-sided. Signs promised things I hadn't thought about needing: "World's Finest Cold Weld!" Little churches beckoned us with clever invitations to salvation: "Forget about Jesus if you can only come to Him weakly." Why will friends-at-a-distance never learn there aren't many cowboys here? Or

conversely, how do they reconcile these rather disparate misapprehensions — that Houston is only slick glass buildings and oil-rich tycoons living in absurd palaces furnished with art they don't understand? And why will those friends never comprehend how it is that, its reputation not withstanding (glitz, crime, roaches, mechanical bulls and the Church of Football, oil wells on every lawn, refinery fires, presidential assassins with telescopic sights on their rifles, a lot of West Texas lope and drawl) — we can already miss it so deeply? ■

Highway 105 Liberty County. Photo © Keith Carter, 1990

"This is the Texas of seep and flood,

not dust and sunlit fire, furtive, lonely, haunting.

It is hard not to believe the stories of ghostly presences

alive and hidden among the trees there."

FOOTE

A CONVERSATION WITH HORTON FOOTE

Horton Foote left Texas in 1933 at age 17 to become an actor. He would return literally and thematically to his hometown of Wharton, 55 miles southwest of Houston, many times during his distinguished career. From his early plays, which were performed live in the beginning years of television, to his nine-play Orphans' Home Cycle, *to his screenplays for film, Foote has maintained an undeniable connection to Texas. His screenplays for* To Kill A Mockingbird *(1962),* Tender Mercies *(1983) and* The Trip to Bountiful *(1985) were honored with Academy Award nominations, with the first two winning the award. His play* Young Man From Atlanta *won the Pulitzer Prize for Drama in 1995.*

Horton Foote lives and works in Wharton, where he met with Terrence Doody and Nonya Grenader on August 5, 1997, for this Cite *interview.*

Cite: We've read that you came to writing in an interesting way. Early in your career, when you were an actor, Agnes De Mille asked if you ever thought about writing.
Foote: That's right. I was quite young and was invited by Mary Hunter to join the American Actors' Company. Members of the company came from all parts of America, and we tried to get each other familiar with our certain regions. We would do improvisations, and I was always doing something about Texas. Agnes had come to do a show with us, and she took me aside and asked, "Have you thought about writing?" When I said, "No, I never have," she said, "You should

think about it. You have interesting material, an instinct, and a sense of place."

At the time, I didn't know what she was talking about. At the time I thought, "Well, doesn't everyone write about Texas?" I just couldn't imagine that seemed peculiar. So, I thought about it and wrote a one-act play called *Wharton Dance.* I knew so little that I used real names of kids I grew up with. We put it on in our own little studio theater, and for some reason Robert Coleman, who was a critic then for the *Daily Mirror,* saw it and liked it a lot, and, of course, I was thrilled.

I was only 22 or 23, and I sent the notice and the play back to my mother. She was so excited about it that she put something in the *Wharton Spectator.* So all of my friends read the play, but they were not too happy because it wasn't all complimentary. I mean, there were girls drinking beer in the play, and they didn't do that in those days — weren't supposed to. I learned the lesson very quickly that, however you did it, you didn't use real names.

Cite: The setting for your early plays was a town called Harrison — a fictional place, but isn't it very similar to Wharton? Also, in many of these plays there is something about the Gulf, the breeze or smell of the Gulf, and other particulars of the Texas landscape.
Foote: It's interesting — I took the name Harrison because my grandfather's name was Albert Harrison Foote. There is a well-known family here named Harrison. They all think I used their name, but I

didn't. Then one day after these early plays had been on television, I got a letter from a lady who said, "I'm very confused. I live in Harrison, Texas, but we have no Gulf breezes." I didn't know until then that there was a real Harrison on the other side of Dallas. But I didn't change it; I decided to stick with it.

Cite: The 1950s were a unique time in television with shows like the "Philco-Goodyear Playhouse" and "Playhouse 90." There was a group of distinguished actors and directors.
Foote: It was an exciting time. We were pioneers in a way because television was live. There was no tape, and it was really quite close to theater, which is why I liked it a lot. There was a group from the Actors' Studio — Lee Strasberg was quite active then, and all of these young actors were coming along: Geraldine Page, Kim Stanley, Julie Harris. They were just starting out, and they were burgeoning, obviously great talents. Same way with the directors: Arthur Penn, Vincent Donehue, and Delbert Mann.

Everybody was defining TV — making it up for themselves. Paddy Chayefsky and I were close friends, but we had a different vision. He wanted to do much more with the cinema — which finally won out because of the economics, not the aesthetics. When the television industry moved out to the coast, it was good-bye; then, the minute they discovered tape, it was another good-bye. With tape they could stop and cut, but you couldn't do that with teleplays — once you started you couldn't stop.

Cite: Was there anybody else in television at the time writing regional things the way you were? How did those regional themes play on national television?
Foote: Well, what happened was budgets were very small for television. And there was a man, who was really a genius, called Fred Coe. He was a producer from Alligator, Mississippi, who decided, since he liked writers a lot and couldn't afford stars, he would make the writer the star. So he featured the writers, really starred us. It was always known as a Horton Foote play or a Paddy Chayefsky play or a Gore Vidal play. So I came along, and it never occurred to me to write about anything else but Texas. Fortunately he was a Southerner, so he was very sympathetic. I had enormous success.

The most important play for me, the one that really upset the apple cart when television came of age, was *The Trip to Bountiful.* That was also because Lillian Gish played the role of Carrie Watts. She hadn't been seen in a while, but she had this tremendous following in America because of her film work.

I hadn't realized the impact of television. The studio was fairly small at NBC. I saw the dress rehearsal in the booth with the technicians, and then I went to see it on the set. When we came out afterward for the reception with the actors, it was an enormous success. William Paley, who was at CBS, said, "Television has come of age tonight." And it was mainly because of Lillian Gish.

Then Kim Stanley had great success in a play of mine called *Young Lady of Property.* I went on and on, but finally I

Left: Horton Foote. Photo by Eric H. Antoniou

just quit because I didn't feel these things were coming very spontaneously out of me and my experiences and what I thought about this place. I felt I would begin to repeat.

Cite: It must have been interesting for you to take *Trip to Bountiful* from that teleplay to a stage play.
Foote: And then to film.

Cite: You're known for a certain kind of independence.
Foote: That's right, I'll fight for it. I'll take much less money to keep some measure of control.

Cite: Samuel Freedman of the *New York Times* describes your work as "offering a private kind of pleasure, much like the scrubby, flat landscape of Wharton in winter; ordinary to the itinerant eye but oddly beautiful to one who lingers."
Foote: You know, I've always thought it was beautiful around here. It never occurred to me that one wouldn't. My wife, who passed away five years ago, adored it. She thought it was beautiful, and my children think it's magical. I do like it; there's something very appealing about it.

Cite: If you had never left, how would that have affected your imagination and your sense of this place?
Foote: I've always kept in touch. I'm really a senior citizen out here — one of the last — so I carry a great deal of the history, and people are always calling me about it. But memory can't always be trusted, you know. When I talk to the people who have lived here forever, have never left, I think their sense about the place is different from mine. They may be a little more pragmatic than I am. Most of them have a sense of loss. Part of it is sentimental, I suppose, because, as we know, nothing is going to stay the same. I don't know quite the way I rationalize it.

For instance, when I was young the street my grandparents' house was on was called Quality Hill, and the houses were just fantastic. When I think of how it is now, I have a surge of anger. But then I think, "Well, that's ridiculous. It's happened all over America." I would have been too young to do anything about it, but the people here have viewed it as a great loss. The street this house was on was called Richmond Road. When I grew up it was gravel, and it took four or five hours to get to Houston. Often it was so muddy you couldn't get there at all. But

when the highway was paved, and they took the highway to the coast, there was a big debate about whether to bypass the town. The merchants were against it, said it would kill Wharton, that people would never trade in Wharton again, and they won out. And I remember the advent of the car and when the first filling station was built on this street. I suppose they thought it was progress.

The other thing that defined the town back then was the invention of the cotton machine. I was carrying on about the cotton machine, and someone asked "Did you ever pick cotton?" I said, "Well, no." They said, "If you had gone in that field and picked cotton you would understand the cotton machines." My father had a store. I worked with him, and we would open the store from 7 in the morning to 11 at night on Saturday because that was a day of great celebration — everyone coming in from the fields. Now you go into town on Saturday, and no one is there. I've long since stopped being upset by it. I just observe and say, "This is how it is."

Cite: So much of your work is about change, about characters coming to terms with those changes.
Foote: Yes, what else are you going to do? I still keep a place in New York, and I was walking down Hudson Street in Greenwich Village when someone asked me, "Did you know the Hudson River used to be here, and they've filled it all in?" Well, there it is.

Cite: They did it to build tenement houses. How did your family come to Wharton?
Foote: My great-great-grandfather, Albert Clinton Horton, came from Alabama. I've never known how he got here. I think he first went to Matagorda. I don't think he came to Wharton until, well, I know the plantation was built in 1840. He was a very successful planter. He had sugar cane and cotton. I don't know how many acres he had, but a large amount of acreage. He had 120 slaves. You think of what it was like, the slavery, and you almost can't conceive of it. But there it was, and it was not that long ago.

He was first lieutenant governor of Texas, during the Mexican War. The governor went off to war, so he became governor. His portrait is in the rotunda of the Capitol as governor, which he was indeed — at least half a term.

My mother's branch of the family all came from Virginia. They came first to

East Columbia in Brazoria County. And from there my grandfather came to Wharton. The plantation was torn down in the 1950s or 1960s. My branch of the family didn't inherit it. Wharton itself is still an old town, and most of the original families still have land here. Some of their children have stayed; some are farmers, but it's all changed.

Cite: Orphans' Home Cycle, written in the 1970s, is a series of plays based more specifically on your family — parents, grandparents.
Foote: Yes. I didn't know this until about ten years ago, but Shelby Foote and I realized we were kin. Our ancestors — I don't know how many greats ago — were brothers in Virginia. His branch went to South Carolina, then finally to Mississippi. Mine came down to Galveston. The story was that they had a shipping fleet out of Galveston or that they came down to buy and sell cotton, but no one is alive who remembers.

Cite: You mentioned that you know many of the old stories. I've read that you were a good listener as a child; you spoke of a strong oral tradition in the South.
Foote: Yes, I took it all in. People seemed very real to me because of these stories. I was always fascinated by the quirks in families, why one person in a family was successful and another person wasn't. There were vivid storytellers in my family, and it was interesting to listen to them. I was never bored. I sometimes can't believe they're all gone. There are so many things I would like to ask now that I didn't think to ask them — so many things that you get different versions of, and you don't know really which is correct. How much is fantasy and how much is reality, whatever reality is, none of us really knows. It's so subjective.

I didn't live here for a while, but I've always come back to visit. About eight years ago I decided to come back, and it was a very wise decision. In a way I feel like a stranger because the Wharton that I still cherish is obviously not here. There were eight families that controlled everything. They seemed almost, well, immortal. And they're all gone.

Cite: I was recently watching the film *To Kill a Mockingbird*, which you adapted for the screen from Harper Lee's novel. It was such a moving book and film.
Foote: It was interesting because Harper and I are very good friends; we share the same sensibility. I think her Monroeville

has probably changed even more than Wharton, because they weren't able to shoot the film there. They had to shoot it on the back lot at Universal.

Cite: Certain scenes in the film were not in the novel — I remember one on a porch.
Foote: Yes, that was one I invented.

Cite: There were conversations overheard from the inside of the house to the porch and vice versa. One was with the children, in their bedroom, talking about their mother. It seems that could have happened on the porch of this house.
Foote: Well, that's where I got it. See, that was my front bedroom, and I'd go to sleep listening to my mother and father talking on the gallery. My father called it a gallery, my mother called it a porch. I listened to them. If you remember in the novel, the mother is scarcely mentioned, you just don't know what happened to her, and that bothered me. After all these years I asked Harper about it because she never complained about the changes. But in this scene I was able to bring in the mother.

This house was built the year I was born [1916], and I was brought here as a baby. My grandfather built it as a kind of peace offering. My mother and father eloped, and my grandparents weren't speaking to them.

Cite: Did you feel you were out of place when you lived elsewhere?
Foote: Oh, no. For so long my world was the theater, and in a way, my world is still the theater. In some ways I've made an adjustment now. I just have learned to live without the theater. First of all, it's shrinking. But that was my great passion, much more than film. I was just a theater nut. I was either teaching or directing or writing or involved in some way. And that's a very special world. I've never been able to write about the theater. I've tried a couple of times, but my instincts are not there.

Katherine Anne Porter, whom I admire a great deal, thinks — I've never proved this theory, but I have a hunch it's true — that for writers, themes are established by the time you are ten years old. It doesn't mean that you stick in that period of time, but what is going to concern you thematically is somehow mysteriously there. I think she may be right.

Cite: Are there any writers you like who you think are strong writers about their

Mrs. Watts: It's strange how much I had forgotten, Ludie. Pretty soon it'll all be gone. Five years . . . ten . . . our house . . . you . . . me.

Ludie: Yes'm.

Mrs. Watts: But the river will be here. The fields. The woods. The smell of the Gulf. That's what I took my strength from, Ludie. Not from houses. Not from people.

The Trip to Bountiful, 1953

---

sense of place?

Foote: I was thinking of J. F. Powers, who writes a lot of short stories. A practicing Catholic, he writes about Catholics in a wonderful way. I think he's a great writer. Willa Cather was a great writer. Nathaniel Hawthorne was a great writer.

Cite: I've just been teaching Proust, and he is as firmly in the place of his childhood as anybody. By the time he was ten, it was all set.

Foote: Yes, that's right. Well, look at Philip Roth's *Portnoy's Complaint* — there's a man who writes about his milieu — and *Adventures of Augie March* by Saul Bellow about the Jewish experience. One of my favorite novels — a short novel, *Seize the Day*, by Bellow — absolutely comes out of his experience. A writer who is not read much today but at one time was very popular is James T. Farrell, who wrote about Chicago. Most writers I admire have a strong sense of place.

Cite: Did you know Gore Vidal at all?

Foote: Yes.

Cite: I just read his autobiography last month, *Palimpsest*, and was surprised I liked it so much. I was moved by it.

Foote: I was moved by it, too, and also very saddened by it. He's bright, oh so bright, and politically, I usually agree with him. I think he's awfully hard on Bill Clinton, whom I happen to like a lot. I haven't seen Gore in a long time, but there was a time when I did see him quite often, and he was always witty and always nice to be around.

Cite: In your recent play, *Young Man From Atlanta,* you come back to Houston.

Foote: Houston has always been the nearby city because I was raised here. I'm sentimental about Houston, too. Those fantastic oaks. I cannot bear to go down Main Street. It's a trashy street now. Maybe it was never as beautiful as I remember it.

Cite: *Young Man From Atlanta* was not so much about change in Houston but about change thrust upon the characters, about circumstances. If people left Harrison for Houston because of opportunity, do you think these towns and cities can be as resilient as some of your characters?

Foote: I don't think you can predict that. I don't try to do that. I try to take a situation and examine it, almost impersonally, and try not to be sentimental or subjective. I just try to know the truth as it is, of that moment. That's the only kind of truth you can count on, because the truth can fool you. Who would have thought that the morass here would die down, too? Now the filling stations are all closing and moving to another area. Who knows what will happen here with activity moving to the freeway? And who would've thought that there's not a merchant left in downtown Wharton except one, and he lives in Houston and commutes?

Cite: You've talked about how film has changed. Do you have optimism for the independent filmmaker?

Foote: Well, it's very difficult. Increasingly difficult. I just finished a film called *Alone,* which will show at the Telluride Film Festival this September. Now, you almost have to finance through cable. We can thank Mr. Reagan for that, one of the many things he blessed us with. There was a time that there was an antitrust ordinance against the big studios owning the theaters, then he came along and changed all that. Now the studios control everything, and it's very hard for independents. It's getting to be so corporate. Well, it's the same as the publishing of books. It's all getting to be one big conglomerate, like hospitals, to make more money. And that's what's driving the engine. Not that you don't have to make a profit; you do, to stay in business. But when I made those films, particularly those that my wife and I could do together, we could do them for under $2 million. It's very hard to do that today.

I don't know about you, but I have no desire to see any of these new films. I just don't go. It wouldn't do me any good, since we don't have a movie theater here. But I belong to the Academy so every year I'm inundated with videos. I watch as many as I can so I can vote sensibly. I have films that I watch here. I'm very fond of a Japanese filmmaker called Ozu. And I love John Huston's *The Dead.* There's a film called *Jean de Florette* that is very different in style. It isn't that I only like gentle, quiet films — *Jean de Florette* has a lot of melodrama and thrust to it. It's just the sensibility that interests me.

Cite: In addition to your current screenplay and the retrospective of your films at the Telluride Festival, are there other projects?

Foote: I'm also writing my memoirs for Scribner — only the first 16 years. They want me to do Wharton, and I think really more about Wharton than about me.

Cite: You say you still keep an apartment in New York. Do you go there often?

Foote: Well, during *Young Man From Atlanta*, I was there a lot. And when it was nominated for a Tony, I went for that. And I'll go back in October for a bookstore that's opening and wants to feature my books. It just depends on what happens; if I have another play done.

Cite: Are there any other places, large cities or not, that interest you?

Foote: I'm really very provincial that way. I don't think I'm a good traveler. I'm too involved with my work, I guess. Now, when I go to London, which I don't do often, I spend all my time in the theater.

I'd like to go to Ireland, I guess, because of Yeats and people like that. A dear friend of mine was Herbert Berghoff who had a famous acting studio in New York — HB Studio. He was a Jewish refugee from Germany and, even though he spoke English fairly well, he asked me once, "Do you know what it is like to lose your language?" And I think that's partly it. I find myself very insecure — in other words, I don't have any linguistic talents. Somewhere very early on, I got intimidated. There are many people I know and admire that are passionate about learning Italian and Spanish and French, Russian, Japanese, and so on. And the nearest I've gotten is because I'm very fond of Ezra Pound's *Cantos*. And so I do a lot of work on that — trying to figure out something he's talking about. For instance, I don't have any desire to go to Mexico. Something about being away from my language is very frightening to me. Well, that's very provincial, I know.

But, this is interesting, speaking of the Mexican culture. The thing I'm working on now for Universal is dramatizing Laura Ingalls Wilder's *Little House on the Prairie* series. I have a housekeeper who is Mexican and doesn't speak English very well. She's having great trouble getting to be a citizen because of the language barrier — even though she should be, she'd be a fine citizen. And she was in here the other day and said, "Oh, my daughter's reading those books." Her daughter is ten years old, and it's so marvelous for me to think that this child, whose mother can hardly speak English, is an avid reader.

Cite: Those are books with a strong sense of place — my memory is that every other chapter begins: "And then it got colder . . ."

Foote: When they called me about it, I had never seen it on television. I heard it was not very good, and I didn't think I wanted to do them. But I decided to look at them, and I was very impressed. It's not Mark Twain — it's not Huck and it's not Tom — but there's something very honest about them. Don't you think so?

Cite: Absolutely. Wilder's descriptions of the landscape are beautiful.

Foote: When they came down here, right here in this room, I said, "Look, if I do this I'm not going to sentimentalize this. I'm going to somehow find the spirit of these books." I don't know that it's possible, but I'm sure going to try. There's a great quietness about it.

Cite: Music seems to play a critical part in your plays. Is that something that you grew up with?

Foote: Not then. Again, I don't judge, but there was no music culture here. I guess the most complicated music I heard growing up was Ethelbert Nevin. My mother played the piano, my father collected songs like "Goodnight Mr. Elephant" and "My Sweetheart's the Man in the Moon." I was fascinated, though, when I sat on the porch out there and heard music, through the cotton fields two streets over. That's where all the black barbecue joints and barbershops were, and sitting on the porch, I could hear their music. And on the other side you could hear the Baptist church, because they had the windows open, always. I'd hear the hymns over here and the blues over there.

There's a great thing in Charles Ives's music, of which I've gotten very fond and by which I lived when I was working on the *Orphans' Home Cycle*. That music has all these thematic interests. I've gotten very interested in music. Reynolds Price wrote in his introduction to one of my plays that I'm "the most musical of American playwrights." I don't know how he arrived at that, because I never formally studied music. But the structure of music interests me a lot.

Last night, for some reason, I turned on Channel 8, and they're doing a series on the history of rock 'n' roll, and I listened. I don't know what they're talking about. To me, it's a lot of noise. That dates me, doesn't it? I had no relationship to Ives or to John Cage, and now they are my passion. This other music seems almost sentimentally sensuous. They're priding themselves on something where there's not much substance. I know that popular music has always been sentimental.

Cite: Are there poets you like besides Pound?

Foote: I adore him. I love his early work. And he's influenced me because of his brevity and the preciseness of him. Well you can see behind you [gestures to bookshelves] the poets I like — Dylan Thomas, Elizabeth Bishop, Robert Penn Warren . . .

Cite: When you were an actor. . .

Foote: Long time ago . . .

Cite: . . . was there a philosophy during that time — a concept?

Foote: When I first started, I was 15. I decided I was going to be an actor, and I wasn't going to go to college. My parents thought I was too young to make that decision, so I had to wait a year. When I turned 17 they said, "Well, if you still want to go, we can't have you go to New York, you're just too young." So they sent me to Pasadena Playhouse in California, which was a well-known theater school, an outgrowth of what was then called community theater. They taught acting by acting, and the first thing they put me in was a Roman comedy. Well, I had read one Shakespeare play, and it wasn't very helpful. But I survived and got to New York, where I met a woman named Rosamond Pinchot from a famous family. She had been the nun in Max Rinehart's *The Miracle*. I told her I was looking for a job, and she said, "I'm studying with the Russians, and I need a scene partner. Would you be interested?" My Russian teacher had come to America with Michael Chekhov, and they were all disenchanted with politics. It all had an enormous impact on me. They had great scorn for American acting and the commercialism of it. It wasn't called "the method" at that time — that was Lee Strasberg. I worked with him, too, so I became a great believer in method acting. I think it's a wonderful way of training.

Cite: A more realistic way?

Foote: They say that, but what is realism? It's just as much of a discipline as anything else. When you get right down to it, if something has integrity and meaning, I don't think the outward form means very much. I think there can be just as much sham in surrealism or expressionism or whatever. Actually, there's nothing realistic about it, but they go after a certain sense of truth.

Cite: There is a truthfulness in your dialogue.

Foote: Yes, the thing the Russians gave me was a sense of structure. They had enormous respect for plays. Working as an actor, you would work first to find what the overall thrust of the play was about and then break it down into beats or actions or whatever you want to call that. So you began to see that there were bones, and that there was a spine, ribs, and arms, and legs, and how it was all connected. That was the search you made as an actor.

So when I came along as a writer, I instinctively began to do the same thing — looking for structure. As an actor we were taught to ask, What do you want? Why did you come into the room? What is your purpose? So it unconsciously fed that movement towards a sense of structure. I was very grateful because, believe me, by my second play I was known as a promising playwright, and I knew nothing about playwrighting.

Cite: That must have been difficult.

Foote: It was very hard. For about four years it was painful. So I got away from realistic plays and began to work with dancers. I worked with Martha Graham, Jerry Robbins, Agnes De Mille, and Valerie Bettis. Then I went to Washington and started a theater of my own with my wife. Most of my plays during that time could be considered highly experimental. I was trying to find a way to use dance and music and language all together.

Sam Shepard's a playwright who seems to do that in his play *The Tooth of Crime*.

Cite: Do you have other favorite playwrights? I notice John Millington Synge on the shelf there, the Irish playwright.

Foote: I like him a lot. I do have favorites. I'm very, very close to Chekhov. Almost as much for his short stories as his plays.

When I went to Pasadena, I was practically play illiterate. I'd read a lot of novels, and quite fortunately the things I'd read have stood me in good stead. I loved Willa Cather, even as a young boy, and I loved Mark Twain, and I loved *The Forsyte Saga* by John Galsworthy.

But anyway, during my second year in Pasadena, for my birthday, my grandmother came out there. Eva Le Gallienne had just closed at the Civic Rep, and she was on tour with three Ibsen plays. I had never seen Ibsen and never read him. So my grandmother asked if I'd like to go see *Hedda*. I did, and I was transfixed and said, "I want to see all three." So she took me to all three, and that really changed my life. I thought, "That's what I want to do. I want to be a part of that kind of theater." ■

Foote House, Wharton, 1997. Photo by Nonya Grenader

"That was my front bedroom,

and I'd go to sleep listening to my mother and father

talking on the gallery.

My father called it a gallery, my mother called it a porch."

High Plains Farm. Photo © Paula Chamlee, 1994

"The High Plains of the Texas Panhandle
have lured many, but only the hardy have stayed.
The winds can be fierce and unrelenting,
the winters bitter, the rainfall scant,
and neighbors are often few and far between.
The region attracts those
who have a craving for self-sufficiency,
love a challenge, or
are just plain stubborn."

*"Being always at the mercy of the weather,
my father had many years in which he made virtually nothing,
when hail, high winds, drought, or blight stunted the income
along with the flowering heads of wheat."*

High Plains Farm. Photo © Paula Chamlee, 1994

HIGH PLAINS FARM

Paula Chamlee

After having spent 32 years in other places, I returned to my home place on the High Plains of the Texas Panhandle to begin photographing and writing about my family's farm — 1,100 acres that my parents, now in their mid and late eighties, still work all by themselves. Upon arriving on December 5, 1994, I wrote in my journal:

"The weather is changing, as is common here on the High Plains, with quickness and drama — and as we reached the home place, I stepped out of the car, taking in the air that is overwhelmingly sweet, fresh, energizing. The smell of the air is more than a treat for me; it is a treasure from the past that renews itself each time I return. I stood exalted, breathing deeply and listening to the persistent yet melodic roar of the Panhandle winds that sweep the atmosphere clean. And tonight, those winds are bringing tiny bits of moisture, foretelling a possible snowfall. I am welcomed by the smell of the soil from the plowed fields and the smells of the house that seem exactly the same — somehow a comforting reassurance — the odors of a place that describe it beyond vision, describe and recall the

past days of past years, olfactory senses flooding the mind."

The High Plains are geographically different from the rest of Texas. Originally a treeless plain, the western side of the Panhandle is flat, semi-arid, and sparsely populated. The large open spaces are now accented by clumps of trees marking the farms and ranches and few towns dotted about the region. My parents' farm is near the western edge of the Panhandle in Oldham County, only 23 miles from the New Mexico border. The boundaries of Oldham County include 956,160 acres and a population of 2,278. Where my parents' dry-land wheat farm is located, the water table is too low to make irrigation economically feasible, and the oil and gas wells in the Panhandle, with their attendant prosperity, are farther to the north and east. My paternal grandparents, who arrived on an immigrant train from Iowa in 1910, were among the first permanent settlers of this area. My parents, like my grandparents, have called this "God's country" for as long as I can remember.

For many years I gave little thought to the significance of having come from a

small farming and ranching community. It never occurred to me that there was anything out of the ordinary about my life there until much later, after I had traveled extensively in this country and abroad and lived in several large cities. It always surprised me when someone thought that the way I grew up was unusual. I learned that some of those people had never been in a place where they could see an unobstructed horizon for 360 degrees, or in a place where folks seldom, if ever, locked their doors, or in a place where folks brought gifts of food to your house when they heard you were having family or friends come to visit. And they'd never built a hideout in the top of a hay barn or examined the parched, rain-starved earth for the sprouts of a newly planted crop. Almost none had driven a tractor or a wheat truck, heard coyotes howling in the night, or been covered from head to toe in wheat chaff during summer's harvest. They didn't call the midday meal dinner, or believe that a high school graduating class could be as small as mine — there were nine of us.

In this place, we hardly ever saw a

movie (the nearest one being 50 miles away); for entertainment, the community as well as the school put on plays throughout the year. Neighbors spent time, and still spend time, talking to each other and helping each other regardless of age, religion, or other differences. And I don't recall a crime of violence during all of my years growing up there.

Each time I go back, I have that same feeling of being deeply connected to this land, feeling at home in a landscape that appears stark, unforgiving, and inhospitable. Growing up in a sparsely populated rural area, I experienced the joys of a quietness punctuated only by the sounds of nature. Absorbing the sights, sounds, and smells of the High Plains and blending them into a feeling for the life and the land that has formed me has led me to my way of viewing the world through the lens of my camera. ■

Editor's note: These photographs and writings appeared in Chamlee's book, High Plains Farm *published by Lodima Press (Revere, Pennsylvania) in 1996.*

High Plains Farm. Photo © Paula Chamlee, 1994

*"Vehicles from seven different decades
— the 1920s through the 1980s —
are still in use on the farm."*

High Plains Farm. Photo © Paula Chamlee, 1994

*"For a seat, there's a piece of
plywood on top of the
bare metal springs and a tarp
for upholstery. Last spring,
a litter of kittens was born
on the passenger side."*

High Plains Farm. Photo © Paula Chamlee, 1994

*"My dad built all
the barns, outbuildings,
corrals, and fences."*

High Plains Farm. Photo © Paula Chamlee, 1994

*"Everything has changed,
yet everything is the same.
Superficial things change
— a different wallpaper
and some new upholstery,
a dead tree removed,
a fence taken down.
Yet these changes have little
to do with the
enduring spirit of the place."*

High Plains Farm. Photo © Paula Chamlee, 1994

"I've always had a distinct memory of my father
sitting at his desk, quietly reading or doing his accounting by hand.
He still doesn't own a calculator."

"No trees grow naturally on the High Plains
where my parents' farm is located.
Mom and Dad brought every tree
from other areas and
planted them
themselves."

"I asked my father,
'If you had it to do
all over again,
what would you do differently?'
After a long and refelctive pause,
he replied, 'Not a thing.' "

High Plains Farm. Photo © Paula Chamlee, 1994

High Plains Farm. Photo © Paula Chamlee, 1994

THE VALUE OF PLACE

George F. Thompson

What do we mean by *place*? For those of us who can see, place is the visual composite of the history of an environment. And that environment is a combination of natural and cultural features and processes. Geographers, in particular, like to think of place as involving landforms, vegetation, and humanly constructed worlds. The combination of these three components is complicated because the range of human activity is so widespread. Thus the context of individual structures (such as a hospital or house, barn or fence, ball park or industrial park) as well as systems of land division, modes of transportation, and settlement patterns all must be part of what a place ultimately becomes.

The size and scale of a place, of course, vary — from one's living room, for example, to one's community (say, San Antonio), region (say, the Hill Country), state (Texas), nation (the U.S. of A.), continent (North America), and one's planetary home (Earth). Place, therefore, is dependent upon physical space and scale; it is also dependent upon

time and change. In geologic time, everyday change seems to be nonexistent; in human time, everyday change seems to be frantic and pervasive. The nature of one's inquiry will determine in large part the nature of one's conclusions as to what place means and represents.

Place is a valuable way to explain who we are as individuals and who we are as a state and nation. What does an oil rig inside a national wildlife refuge tell us? What does the conversion of a dilapidated downtown into a thriving historic district tell us? We can learn a lot about our collective attitudes, values, and beliefs by viewing the places of everyday existence. It is the job of writers, artists, scholars, and teachers to observe and interpret these places to explain why one place varies from another — why Austin, for example, is like or unlike Madison, Wisconsin, and why Houston is like or unlike Los Angeles.

By understanding the characteristics of a place, we become better-informed citizens, perhaps making us better caretakers of our lands, our communities,

and the flora and fauna of our world. T. S. Eliot astutely observed that "behavior is belief." If this is true, and I believe it is, through the study of place, we can begin to understand why and how Big Bend came to be Big Bend National Park, why and how Wichita Falls changed after the great tornado of 1979, why and how Paula Chamlee's paternal grandparents left the good soils of Iowa for the small Panhandle town of Adrian, Texas, to create their own landscape and their own dream of the good life.

The photographs and words of Paula Chamlee preserve a vital link to the visual record of her parents' High Plains farm. They tell us much about the limitations of the land when water is scarce and much about the value of the human effort to build and create an environment called home. In Paula Chamlee's world, we regain a sense of place — from a small farm that reveals much about Texas life, Texas land, and the human spirit. In her world, we see truth and beauty revealed in common places. ■

Pottery man, Highway 59 near Marshall. Photo by Nonya Grenader, 1997

"What remains is a road that travels through places
rather than simply between them,
disclosing and hiding history like a peep show."

Citgo Station, Highway 59 near Carthage. Photo by Bruce C. Webb, 1997

ROAD TRIP

BLUE STAR* HIGHWAY 59

Bruce C. Webb

*During World War II, families of those on active duty
in the armed forces displayed a blue star on their front doors.
When a highway collected a certain number of starred houses,
it was designated a Blue Star Highway.*

Like many immigrants coming to Texas in the 1970s from the rust-bucket cities of the Northeast in search of better prospects amid the bountiful newness of Houston, I entered the Lone Star State by way of Texarkana on an oppressively hot August afternoon, leaving the predictable precincts of Interstate 30 to search for U.S. 59 — the last leg of my trip to the Bayou City. Texarkana in the 1970s was a confusing little metroplex for long-distance travelers seeking Houston, mystification compounded by the fact that Texarkana is really two towns in two different states — a situation forever encrypted in its name, which according to legend was assembled by combining three letters from the names of three adjoining states, Texas, Arkansas, and Louisiana (TEX-ARK-ANA). After two days of steady 70-mile-per-hour progress on a series of interstates, navigating the city streets linking I-30 with the inauspicious headwaters of Highway 59 was a challenge. Today that transition has been greatly simplified by the extension of a freeway spur that intersects I-30, keeping through traffic from having any real, direct contact with the city. But the 294-mile run from Texarkana to Houston remains the main route of the hillbilly diaspora from East Texas to Houston that occurred during the Depression and World War II, an imperfect link in the chain of federal highways that have reshaped the way Americans travel.

Before the interstate system, a road map was an essential companion for planning a road trip. Gasoline companies gave plenty of them away to lure Americans out onto the highways and byways. More than simply a navigating device, a map populates distance with adventure and anticipation. Maps also serve as remarkable historical documents, showing in abstract, graphic form the inexorable evolution of the nation's connective tissue. In contrast to the road maps of a few generations ago with their bewildering, ad hoc networks of egalitarian capillary highways, a modern map is distinctly hierarchical and portrays the entire country in abbreviated form. Bold blue ribbons of interstate highway bridge the murky and more slowly evolving spaces in between, linking together a nation of anonymous interchanges.

It is difficult to say how the politics of road building left Houston so poorly connected to the Northeast. The road map depicts Highway 59 as a wandering sequence of several different road configurations generally following a steep northeasterly trajectory that threads its way through dozens of small and medium-sized towns like a child's connect-the-dots puzzle. Portions of the road remain two-lane, while newer sections bypass cities such as Livingston and Lufkin with a limited-access modern freeway. For the most part, the highway is shaped in four-lane sections in narrow rights-of-way created by slicing off front yards of homesites, businesses, and farmsteads (usually on the west side) and grafting two new lanes onto the old two-lane road. The result puts the highway uncomfortably close to the buildings fronting it and makes the driver feel like an intruder into the sanctum of adjacent domestic life. Kids frolic in thin front yards, while traffic zips by at posted speed limits of 70 miles per hour. Even new houses follow the awkward building line. On-grade crossings and driveway entrances to adjacent properties are frequent, creating the need for constant vigilance.

Wooded landscape is characteristic along most of the run through East Texas, which passes close by several national forests and lakes. Huge stands of pines shape the right of way, opening up here and there like a theater curtain to views of trailer parks, model homes, small factories, and an occasional picturesque vista.

Just south of Splendora the highway begins its final assault on Houston. Fleshing out to near-interstate design standards and colonized by giant car dealerships, it enters the city to become an important part of the metropolitan circumferential and radial freeway system. Rush-hour drivers are treated to billboards inviting homebuyers to move out to Kingwood.

Highway 59 lacks the ambition of I-10 (Jacksonville to Los Angeles) or the romance of I-45 (Galveston to Dallas), the two other long-distance freeways that converge on Houston. It enters the central city on the east side, sliding along the backside of the George R. Brown Convention Center as the Eastex Freeway, and leaves as the Southwest Freeway bound for Sharpstown, Sugar Land, and points beyond. Its progress is marked by places full of history whose names memorialize their earliest settlers. Unlike the interstate highways, which are self-referentially structured like a sonnet sequence (so many mileage markers to an interchange; so many interchanges to the next city), distances along 59 are apt to be existentially defined (the Dairy Queen sign announces, "BE THERE IN TWO SHAKES"). Signage, as befits its proximity to the road, is generally small and often hand painted, and whatever is advertised is usually delivered close at hand.

Although there are plenty of examples of the selfsame chain motels, eateries, and filling stations that congregate around interstate interchanges, much of the road architecture along Highway 59 is a product of hometown builders improvising modest interpretations of familiar formulas. A common version of the gas-station-cum-convenience-store is a log cabin or vernacular houselike building mated to a stand of gasoline pumps, a rough and artless configuration somewhere between a general store of a previous generation and the patterns of a modern convenience store. Each is one of a kind and, with residential-scale windows rather than walls of plate glass, they hide their interiors, engendering a sense of discovery as well as anxiety about conditions within. There are always a few locals hanging around inside, some of them conjuring up memories of scenes from the movie *Deliverance*. With little in common to bridge the gap between travelers and locals, conversation is restrained and usually limited to func-

Country Cottage, Highway 59 near Marshall. Photo by Bruce C. Webb, 1997

tional exchanges. Along with the partially filled racks of familiar candy bars and junk food and a varnished plywood snack bar, there are usually some unique local finds: Saran-wrapped homemade candies, gimme caps, souvenirs, and trinkets, all of which seem to have had too long a shelf life.

Junk shops and antique stores appear that look like Kienholz installations, cobbled together from old buildings and garnished with vast collections of hand-me-downs that seem to have overflowed the interior, spilling out helter-skelter onto the parking lot. A cluster of quilt shops, with samples on clotheslines flapping in the compression breezes produced by passing cars and 18-wheelers, are almost within touching distance of the road. And purveyors of the homegrown and the homemade — boiled peanuts, watermelons, pecans, and the mysterious mayhaw jelly — conduct business out of the back of pickup trucks parked along the berm or from ramshackle sheds. In places where the concessions group together, the effect is like traveling at highway speeds through a continuous, less-than-grand bazaar.

Sometimes these roadside concoctions are remarkably ambitious. The Dinosaur Park, operated by Don and Yvonne Bean just outside the little town of Moscow, was the fulfillment of Don Bean's dream of creating a park similar to one he saw many years ago in Oregon. Investing their life savings from careers in carpentry and real estate, the Beans made a deal with sculptor Bert Holster, who creates fiber-

glass figures for commercial purposes, to produce large models of dinosaurs based on drawings the couple made from encyclopedia research. The garden opened some 18 years ago, about the time the animated dinosaurs were drawing big crowds to science museums around the country. The Beans' Dinosaur Park exudes unscientific quaintness; the folksy dinosaur figures are slipped into a vernal setting, more like a back yard than a theme park, of natural landscaping, where they reside in a perpetual tableau vivant. Hidden speakers fill the air with recorded animal roars and growls, and little hand-painted signs spring up along the path bearing not just specimen labels but folk tales and religious messages as well. It's a true work of folk art, naively ambitious and charmed, although the Beans, who see their park as a commercial enterprise, would probably have it otherwise.

The modern American highway has drastically altered the ritual of dining, turning it into a food form mass-marketed to people on the run. The menus, centering around burgers, fries, and anything that can be turned into morsels of deep-fried crunch, have become an international phenomenon, with the same fast food found under the Golden Arches close to home and in Moscow's Pushkin Square. The result is that a day's travel to any distant destination always brings you into familiar territory when it's time to eat. Kids in particular begin to salivate at the sight of advertising stimuli planted in their heads by television ads, and their

parents know that inside they will encounter a familiar, hassle-free eating experience. The restaurant-chain industry has broadened its target to include items for the health conscious, as well as post-modernized versions of international dishes. It also created the restaurant-as-horn-of-plenty by mating incidental steak entrées with vast, all-you-can-eat buffet bars patronized by diners who understand that gluttony must be one of the unwritten provisions of the Bill of Rights.

Highway 59 has all of these modern variations in abundance, and the traveler looking for something different has to get off the main road around the town in hopes of discovering restaurants of the *genius loci*. But it can be disconcerting to find that there are few rubes left in the restaurant business; most of them have taken a lesson or two from their more modern competitors, who are marketing not just food but the idea of food. At a motel in Lufkin we learned about a local place called Buck's Mesquite Grill from the woman working the desk, who promised a unique dining experience — wild game served up in an appropriate atmospheric setting. We set out to find Buck's, which turned out to be a road-house-looking place, newly built, tucked into the folds along the bypass road. Buck's was an amateur version of a theme restaurant, a kind of second or third-generation simulation, and the kind of place that creates its own legend de novo. The theme here was hunting lodge — a stage-set interior constructed of rough-sawn lumber and decorated with taxidermy,

the atmosphere thickened with the sweet smell of burning mesquite. "Buck's Tale," printed in the menu, tells the story of how "Buck sets out into the crowded pines with the bare necessities of gear: his .308 Winchester and a box of cartridges, his Buck journal filled with scribbled locations of recent rubs and scrapes, and his devoted hound, Ol' Jet." That evening, back at the lodge, Buck recounts his hunt to the sportsmen. And knowing that hunters cultivate intense appetites, Buck offers only the finest provisions for his friends — steaks, venison, chicken, and seafood, all grilled over hot mesquite. Outfitters supply the hunters with buckets of homemade jalapeño cheese corn muffins and all-you-can-eat salad. "Finally, as the evening concludes, the hunters settle up with Buck. A no-non-sense man, he only accepts even bucks because he knows sportsmen don't want the jingle of change in their pockets to startle their prey. To keep things simple, tax is included in each meal. No change, no worries."

Our waiter, who introduced us to Buck's menu by writing entrées on the paper tablecloth with crayons, told us that they had some antelope left, but the venison was all gone until a new shipment arrived from Denver. So much for the illusion of local game. He also inquired if we had been sent over from the motel, and unabashedly told us that they get a lot of referrals from his girlfriend at the desk there, paying her two dollars a head. So much for the sense of discovery. This is the land of big eating — king-size steaks,

Dinosaur Gardens, Highway 59 near Moscow. Photo by Bruce C. Webb, 1997

Junktique, Highway 59 near Carthage. Photo by Bruce C. Webb, 1997

all-you-can-eat fried catfish, biscuits, grits — and a feature of every Buck's meal was the biggest baked potatoes I have ever seen, which we were invited to garnish with 11 food substances laid out at the Buckboard bar. Salad and biscuits came in paper tubs tucked inside galvanized buckets, a sanitized version of the the way the outfitters in Buck's Tale served them. Like a familiar symphony played by the local town band, Buck's was learning how to turn local culture into hyperreality.

Like the interstate system, which has forever forsaken the old roads through town and their dilapidated, family-run motels and restaurants, Highway 59 is now shaped by a series of bypasses that divert traffic around attractive little downtowns. Or at least they were attractive before the bypasses became the new Main Streets: messy fringe-strip districts where Wal-Mart rules over an endless jumble of chaotic parking lots, fast-food emporiums and other drive-up establishments, new chain motels, and an occasional home-grown imitator. In county seats such as Marshall, a handsome courthouse still sits stoically in the well-formed town square, its buildings now largely abandoned (including the impressive, 12-story Marshall Hotel). The only extant occupants are law offices, antique stores, and an occasional family-owned restaurant. It is difficult to imagine that anyone could have consciously planned the mass exodus from these socially commodious town squares for the free parking out in the non-place realm on

the perimeter.

Other towns harbor rich troves of fine historic architecture, some of it in well-preserved residential districts. Nacogdoches, which bills itself as "the oldest town in Texas," has several visitable sites attesting to its complex and colorful history: a Caddo Indian mound; a replica of the old stone fort built by the Spanish in 1779; the remaining stone structure of Old Nacogdoches University, chartered in 1845; and many fine old houses. Farther north and west of Highway 59 is the city of Jefferson, formerly an inland port where, for a brief period in the late 19th century, steamboats arrived from the Mississippi by way of a route that linked Big Cypress Bayou to Caddo Lake and the Red River. The Army Corps of Engineers dismantled the arrangement by dynamiting a jam of debris in the Red River in 1874, making the channel impassable for steamboats. Jefferson has capitalized on its historic resources, refashioning itself as a living museum by restoring much of its historic downtown, including the Excelsior Hotel, the second-oldest hotel in Texas, filling the empty shops with antique stores, and carefully refurbishing many large old homes, most of which have been converted into bed and breakfasts. With its proximity to Caddo Lake State Park, Jefferson's aggressive promoters see a bright future for the town as a tourist mecca, luring nostalgia buffs, sportsmen, and ecotourists.

In a series of little towns that includes Garrison and Timpson, Highway 59, at

four lanes, still forms one of the sides of the town squares, with big pot-bellied water towers in the background serving to mark the town sites. Tenaha, which has its own stoplight as well as a rare case of civic boosterism, advertises itself as "A Little Town With Big Potential" and still has a functioning "Whistle Stop" restaurant across the street from the small, amazingly adept neoclassical town hall. In a bleak declaration of egocentrism, a sign on a blank brick wall graphically proclaims Tenaha to be the center of a cosmos consisting of the surrounding towns of Timpson, Carthage, Joaquin, and Center. Tenaha is also the location of Loop 168, Texas's shortest state highway (395 feet), a fact commemorated on a plaque honoring E. H. Wall, "one of our pioneer civic leaders who was instrumental in obtaining Texas Loop 168 so the square of Tenaha could be paved."

The progression along Highway 59, with its time-killing inconsistencies, can be annoying to the traveler hell-bent on simply getting there. But what makes it a road still worth coping with are precisely the cracks and breaks that keep it so incomplete. They become the portals through which one peers into a life that is vanishing. You can sense the new squeezing out the old, but there has never been enough prosperity or enough trade to finish the job. What remains is a road that travels through places rather than simply between them, disclosing and hiding history like a peep show. Inevitably the new will eat the old. Already there is serious talk about a new highway, Interstate 69,

that would roughly follow the present 59 alignment to link the Tex-Mex border with Chicago, supporting the commercial potentials of the North American Free Trade Agreement. When this occurs, another layer of history and another place of discovery will be bypassed, burying the sense of place under new signs of progress. The Beans' Dinosaur Park and dozens of careworn little businesses and struggling motels along the old road show that progress is always gained at the expense of someone else's dreams. And in these easy few steps we estrange ourselves from sources of knowing who we are and where we came from. It is perhaps inevitable, but nevertheless a little sad to see. ■

RIDING THE SUNSET

Margaret Culbertson

"You have to *want* to live out here," says the man across the table from me.

I'm on the Sunset Limited heading west, sitting at a table with white tablecloth and napkins in air-conditioned comfort, insulated from the noises of the tracks and the engines, gliding smoothly through a stark, impressive West Texas landscape. We had passed through Marfa at the beginning of dinner, and now, with dessert before us, the landscape has changed. There is less grass, less mesquite, less of any kind of visible plant material, yet we continue to see animals, including deer, antelope, and a jackrabbit. Suddenly, the tiny, ramshackle community of Valentine appears outside the window. It was probably never a thriving town, but today it looks almost deserted, with most houses in bad repair and several abandoned to the elements. No humans are visible, but a lone cow is standing calmly in the middle of a deserted street, chewing its cud and watching the train go by. "You have to *want* to live out here," says the man across the

table, a native of El Paso.

He is undoubtedly right. Life is not easy in this part of West Texas. It takes acres of land to feed one cow, and the annual rainfall will not support much in the way of traditional agriculture. Towns are few, small, and very far between. But the scale of the land is grand, with mountains often visible in the distance. For those burdened by crowded cities and suburban sprawl and who are comfortable with their own company, this land is heaven and worth the trouble.

As a temporary respite from those same crowded cities and sprawling suburbs, there is no more comfortable way than the train to enjoy these vast landscapes. No worry about staying awake at the wheel and no cramped muscles from hours of confinement in an automobile seat. However, as I sit transfixed by the moving panorama outside my window, it occurs to me that there is a similarity between the harsh West Texas landscape and cushioned train travel across Texas. You also have to want to take the train. Travel times are long, the trains are often

late, and the scheduled departure and arrival times, falling, as they do, in the middle of a transcontinental run, are not designed for the convenience of Texas residents. If you want to ride the train from Houston to El Paso, the scheduled travel time is 17 hours and one minute, and you have to be prepared to leave Houston at one minute before midnight. There are no other choices. You can choose from three days of the week, Sunday, Wednesday, or Friday, but there is no choice in the time. One minute before midnight.

Personally, I found the idea of a midnight departure on the train exciting, and I embarked upon the Sunset Limited with great anticipation and a fair amount of mental baggage, including some of the extensive legend and lore about both the Sunset Limited and West Texas, memories of travel on other trains, both actual and from the movies, and fairly distant memories of a few automobile trips across West Texas.

I have ridden and enjoyed trains in Europe and on the East Coast corridor

between Washington, D.C., New York, and Boston, but I am not a train buff, and I am woefully ignorant of much of the history and workings of trains in America. For example, for many years, it never occurred to me that train tracks belonged to specific railroad companies. If I thought about it at all, I probably assumed that railroad tracks were like highways, open to anyone with a diesel engine. Now, thanks to a good, train-literate friend, I know that the tracks that run by the Katy Freeway originally belonged to the MKT (Katy) Railroad Company, and that the tracks with the traffic-stopping grade crossing on Richmond, near the Galleria, now belong to the Union Pacific. The business of track ownership had seemed like a piece of interesting but esoteric trivia until the Amtrak Sunset Limited stopped before we reached San Antonio and waited on a siding for a freight train to pass. As we waited in the stillness, I was reminded that, since Amtrak doesn't own the tracks over which it runs, there are times when it must give way to the owner's freight trains.

Left: **The Sunset Limited at the San Antonio station.** Photo by Margaret Culbertson, 1997

Mountain east of El Paso. *Photo by Margaret Culbertson, 1997*

This trip gave me the opportunity to improve my understanding of trains, as well as to reacquaint myself with the West Texas landscape. I am a native Texan, but it has been years since I have ventured west of Castroville or the Hill Country. In fact, living more than 20 years in Houston's subtropical greenness has made even the Blackland Prairie near Dallas, where I spent much of my youth, seem somewhat alien, to say nothing of the wide desert expanses of West Texas.

However, watching those wide expanses through the train windows is what made this trip memorable. I spent hour after hour in the observation car, kept impolitely glancing out the windows during dinner conversations, and stared out the window of my compartment with an unread book on my lap. The views were not traditionally beautiful and did not match stereotypical desert images, but they held my attention nonetheless.

Part of the fascination lay in the gradual transformation of the landscape as we progressed and the realization that one could actually see that transforma-

tion in spite of the length of time, or number of miles, over which it occurred. Watching the subtle alterations of the shapes, textures, and colors of the land and its flora was almost like watching an organic growth process, similar in a way to a time-lapse film of seeds sprouting upward. The land would slowly flatten or develop hillocks or crevices, mountains and geologic formations would emerge or disappear, mesquite would cover the ground or thin out to reveal innumerable yucca plants, all in bloom after the July rains. The infinite slow-motion variations captured my attention and wouldn't let go.

Before this panorama could material-ize before us, we had to board the train in Houston and pass through hours of darkness on the way to San Antonio. The Houston Amtrak station is anything but an inspiring setting for the beginning of a rail journey across the State of Texas. Built in the 1960s and stuck between the Houston police garage and the downtown post office, the tiny, non-descript station is surrounded by

reminders of the automobile's victory over passenger trains. The building sits literally in the shadow of an elevated portion of Interstate 45; mail trucks con-stantly rumble past the tracks that once carried the bulk of the mail entering or leaving the city. No grand portals frame the entrance to the platform, and the atmosphere of the station's interior is more like a small bus station than the gateway to the legendary Sunset Limited.

The Sunset Limited made its first run in 1894, connecting New Orleans and San Francisco. It was advertised as the "quickest, safest, and pleasantest route to the coast," a preferable alternative to the northern route that might "carry you into the heart of the Rockies and leave you there a week or more, snow-bound."[1] It was a deluxe train, with the most modern cars and luxurious accom-modations possible, including gas chan-deliers and potted palms. There was even a separate "ladies' compartment car," attended by a maid and including a par-lor and a library. In 1912, the western terminus was changed to Los Angeles,

and now Amtrak has extended the run east to Miami, making the route a true transcontinental link.

The current Amtrak Sunset Limited cars may not be as elegant as their chan-delier-hung predecessors, but they are undoubtedly much more comfortable. The ride is smooth, and effective sound-proofing cuts out almost all track and engine noise. The seats are more comfort-able and roomier than you will find in the coach class of any airplane, and the dining is far more civilized. However, it was the size of the cars that surprised me first when the train pulled into the Houston station, dwarfing the clusters of passengers waiting to board. The entire train is essentially a tall double-decker, with seating and sleeping compartments on two levels, but with passage between cars only on the upper level. The dining car has seating on the upper level and the kitchen on the lower level, while the lounge car has observation windows and seating on the upper level and a snack bar and tables below.

The situation on the platform when

Irrigated field east of El Paso. Photo by Margaret Culbertson, 1997

the train arrived seemed chaotic compared to the regimented channeling of passengers in airports. The minimal local staff offered no directions or controls, and the waiting passengers surrounded the few uniformed personnel descending from the arriving train. I was eventually directed to one of the two sleeping cars at the far end of the train and found my compartment on the lower level.

It was a tiny space with room for only the two seats it contained, one facing the other, with the dark window in between. For privacy from those passing in the corridor, one could either slide a door or pull a curtain. The two seats could be folded out to form the lower berth, and an upper berth pulled down from above. "Deluxe Bedrooms" with sinks and toilets are available for an additional fee, as well as "Family Bedrooms" with two adult-sized berths and two smaller berths, and "Accessible Bedrooms" designed for passengers with special mobility requirements. Even though my compartment was small, it felt luxurious to stretch out between

starched sheets in the moving train, hearing the train's whistle, filtered through the insulated wall, sounding as distant as the train whistles I hear in my own house at night.

Sleep was impossible while the train was passing familiar sights and streets on its way out of the sleeping city. The circuitous route we were following required continuous attention. In fact, it took the daylight return trip to clarify the unexpected twists and turns. Although our next stop was San Antonio, we were not on the tracks that run alongside Interstate 10 on its way to the same destination. We wound north and south, crossing I-10 twice while still inside Loop 610, then headed south through Memorial Park, under the Southwest Freeway, through Bellaire, and eventually out of town alongside South Main Street, passing by Missouri City and Sugar Land. The tracks even took us by the gates of the state prison farm in Sugar Land, where Huddie Ledbetter, also known as Leadbelly, spent time as a prisoner in the 1920s. He undoubtedly heard the whis-

tles of passing night trains like ours, and he included references to the Sugar Land prison in his recordings of the blues classic "Midnight Special."

The route of the Sunset Limited reflects history rather than the straight line of a ruler. When C. P. Huntington of the Southern Pacific Railway decided to extend his line east from California, he made a deal with Thomas Pierce of the Galveston, Harrisburg & San Antonio Railway to use that company's existing tracks between Houston and San Antonio. The two companies laid track from opposite directions across West Texas and met in 1883 at a spot 227 miles west of San Antonio. These businessmen selected routes with the greatest revenue potential, connecting existing towns rather than looking for the shortest path between large cities, although they did create a few new towns at locations where the steam engines required water. Consequently, the Sunset Limited still heads southwest from Houston through Richmond, west through Eagle Lake, then northwest through Columbus

before finally settling into a more straightforward westward line towards San Antonio. After San Antonio, the tracks go almost due west to Del Rio before turning northwest through Sanderson, Alpine, Marfa, Sierra Blanca, and finally El Paso. Being a limited, the train stops only at San Antonio, Del Rio, Sanderson, and Alpine.

On my trip west, after San Antonio, the morning light illuminated a series of similar small towns whose water towers communicated their identity: Hondo, D'Hanis, Sabinal, Knippa, Uvalde. Yellow wildflowers lined the tracks and occupied entire fields between the towns. After Del Rio, the wide expanses of the Amistad Reservoir, created in 1968 by damming the Rio Grande, interrupted the progressively more desertlike landscape through which we had been traveling.

Crossing the high bridge 321 feet above the deep canyon of the Pecos River provided one of the most dramatic sights of the trip. The original route crossed more to the south, where the Pecos joined the Rio Grande, but even that crossing was difficult, requiring tunnels through

Ranch west of Del Rio. Photo by Margaret Culbertson, 1997

the cliffs on both sides of the bridge. To shorten the route and reduce the grades required by that early crossing, Jim Converse, a Southern Pacific engineer, envisioned a long "high-line viaduct that will skip the descent into the Pecos Canyon altogether, and practically swing the railroad through the clouds."[2] Completed in 1892, the bridge was the third highest in the world for many years. It was replaced by a cantilevered steel structure in 1944.

After the Pecos River the land rolled in billows like the sea. Mesquite- and sage-brush-covered billows gradually increased in size, with the path of the train cutting directly through some of them, exposing layers of geological history. Mountains began to appear as we neared Sanderson, and some of them, surprisingly, seemed to be covered in a thin film of green velvet. I learned that July is the beginning of the rainy season here, and instead of the brown desert I was expecting, the land was filled with yellow wildflowers, green bushes, blooming yucca, and ditches full of standing water.

After Alpine we crossed Paisano Pass, the highest point of the route at 5,074 feet. The altitude of the pass was a surprise, for the train never seemed to be climbing during the trip. For most of our time in the Trans-Pecos region the mountains remained in the distance, but at Paisano Pass, impressive rock formations and rocky slopes briefly approached the train before withdrawing again to a discreet distance.

On the long stretch between the Pecos River and Sierra Blanca, occasional reminders of the cattle industry's influence on this area's history and legend came into view: isolated windmills and water troughs, a few houses with corrals, cattle pens by the tracks in the towns, even a few cows roaming the range. But traces of mankind were few in this area where land and sky and distant mountains dominated every vista. It was, therefore, almost shocking when, west of Marfa and Valentine, a lush, irrigated orchard appeared on the south side of the tracks, like a mirage. For miles, the tracks formed the dividing line between vast

expanses of desert and this unlikely area of agricultural productivity. Nearing El Paso, irrigated fields became more frequent, but the contrast with the surrounding desert remained unsettling.

El Paso's train station, in contrast to Houston's, is a fitting structure to welcome a weary traveler, at least aesthetically. Built in 1905, the red-brick station was designed by Daniel H. Burnham & Co. of Chicago. It is finely detailed, with a generous, full-height central waiting room. The City of El Paso obtained grant funds to restore the building in the mid-1980s, removing white paint and other traces of the 1940s attempt to convert it to the Spanish Colonial style, and the city's Public Transport Administration now occupies part of the structure. Since so few passenger trains actually stop at the station, service facilities consist only of vending machines and two pay telephones, but the design and generous proportions of the space serve as a reminder of the station's more vibrant days.

All surviving train stations in Texas are reminders of a world that no longer

exists, whether they still serve occasional trains or have been converted to banks or antique stores. Rail remains important in the state, but passenger trains are an anomaly, and freight rules the tracks. The situation is not inevitable — rapid, efficient train service can be found in countries around the world. But, in Texas at least, you have to make a special effort to take the train, changing your schedule to conform to its schedule and remaining patient with occasional delays. However, our train was filled with people who had done just that.

Heading west, there was a grandmother from California giving her grandchildren a Great American Train Ride around the country; a Los Angeles woman who had visited Louisiana to see the rural communities where her parents had grown up; and a couple from Florida celebrating their 25th wedding anniversary with a trip to California and the Midwest. Heading home to Houston, I met two retired schoolteachers returning from a vacation in California; a woman from North Carolina returning from a visit

Alpine. Photo by Margaret Culbertson, 1997

with her brother in Arizona; and an oil company executive from San Antonio returning from a conference in Canada. All had interesting stories to tell.

A retired couple from Florida, whom I met at lunch on the trip west, were amazed, when I showed them my map, at how much of Texas remained to be traversed. It is easy to forget the grand scale of this state when we fly from one city to another. Trains, however, enable us to savor distances and use them to expand our knowledge or relax our tensions.

Late at night, in my berth, on the trip back to Houston, I was listening to the train whistle and staring at the darkness when a curve in the tracks changed the train's direction slightly and brought the moon floating into my vision. The tracks curved again and it floated away, but a few minutes later it moved slowly to the exact center of the window before drifting away for the last time. It is said that the first star, not the moon, grants wishes. But I made a wish on that floating moon that somehow we can keep passenger trains rolling across Texas. ■

1. Arthur D. Dubin, *Some Classic Trains* (Milwaukee: Kalmbach Publishing Co., 1964), p. 198.

2. Neil C. Wilson, *Southern Pacific: The Roaring Story of a Fighting Railroad* (New York: McGraw Hill, 1952), p. 78.

Freeport. Photo by Barrie Scardino, 1997

MOST OF THE COAST
Sabine Pass to Boca Chica

Boca Chica. Photo by Barrie Scardino, 1997

Aransas Pass Lighthouse. Photo by Barrie Scardino, 1997

Barrie Scardino

The coast of anywhere is easy to romanticize — the sounds of crashing waves and sea birds, the smell and taste of salty air, the sun setting across shimmering water. In perfect weather — when there hasn't been a recent oil spill — you can find such idyllic scenes on the Gulf Coast of Texas. But most of the coast is a different story.

My journey along the 367-mile (624, if you count the bays) Texas coastline began with the idea that I would proceed southward from an exotic Cajun/Confederate culture with genteel porticoed architecture to a lively Mexican culture with brightly colored, flat-roofed buildings, faded from the bleaching sun. While these stereotypes have some validity, far more striking was the sameness of it all — top to bottom.

The Texas coast has no equivalent of Newport or Palm Beach. Nor is there a five-star Ritz resort with swim-up pool bars and Fazio-designed golf courses. Texas's beaches and intracoastal waterways provide vacationing families with fresh air and space, birds and fish, and they provide coastal residents with a slow but generally satisfying living. Ethnically the coast does change, but culturally it is

all like a baseball game — a sea-level playing field.

Riding into Port Arthur behind the haunches of an oil truck, I felt like a Guelph (or was it a Ghibelline?) riding into San Gimignano when, around a wide bend in the forest-lined back road, a skyline of oil refinery towers suddenly loomed up in the distance. This was the first clue that the coast of Texas from Sabine Pass to Boca Chica is dominated as much by the oil and petrochemical industry as it is by salt water and sand. To reach Sabine Pass, I drove through a gigantic web of refinery pipes and catwalks on the edge of Port Arthur.

Across the causeway, I stopped at Big Earl's in Sabine Pass for iced tea. Aging Big Earl signs, like the old sequential Burma Shave roadside ads, led me there. Big Earl's was a sad case — the gas pumps were empty, and a 25-watt bulb lit the rickety wooden store, where the stock was pretty low. Miss Betty was frying up chicken while an ingénue with blue nail polish guarded the cash register. Conversation came easy; I learned that Sabine Pass was the victim of a storm seven or so years ago that washed out the road to the Bolivar Peninsula and

Galveston. A lot of vacationers used to come through, but now no one does. The houses and stores of Sabine Pass (pop. 1,500) are weathered and broken, many boarded up, and there was no evidence of new construction. Those who remained on the peninsula worked in the refineries and oil-related companies back toward Port Arthur, but the tourist industry is clearly dead, except for me. I got directions to the state park listed in the guidebooks and said good-bye.

At the foot of the Texas-Louisiana border, which follows the Sabine River through Sabine Lake and out to the Gulf of Mexico at Sabine Pass, sleepy marshes give way to the oil industry. There the Sabine Pass Battleground State Historical Park marks the site where 47 Confederates with only six cannons kept what seemed to have been the whole Union navy and army from invading Texas. The Dick Dowling Monument, the old Fort Griffin bunkers, and five historical markers looked inconsequential next to the offshore-rig construction site next door. The parking lot was empty, as were the RV hookup sites. A long, flat oil tanker, *Al Debaran*, glided eerily by on its way to the sea with no crew visible, as if the

Port Arthur. Photo by Barrie Scardino, 1997

Port Mansfield. Photo by Barrie Scardino, 1997

tall, still cranes on deck were running the ship. This close encounter created the only excitement I felt here, with the possible exception of reading the unlikely tale of the brave Kate Dorman and her Catfish Hotel, which stood on this site in 1847. The other history is military. This is the case all the way down the coast.

With few exceptions, historical markers along the coast tell stories of obscure heroes of the Mexican War (1840s), the Civil War (1860s), and the Spanish-American War (1890s). A lot of fighting took place on every part of the Texas shore, beginning, some say, with the cannibal Indians who ate interloping Spanish explorers. Jean Laffite and other notorious pirates also made bloodcurdling contributions to Texas coast lore. But all those ghosts were hard to feel, except perhaps among the draping live oaks around Matagorda Bay. Otherwise, the spirits of bloody marshes must have drifted away with nothing to hang onto in the empty, flat coastal plain that runs along the rest of the coast.

Highway 87 (the washed-out one), led to an almost deserted Sea Rim State Park. The chatty attendant confirmed that the beaten path had moved elsewhere. But because the park is uncrowded and has nice beaches with campsites, self-guided nature trails through the wetlands, plus hot showers, it would be a good place to come back to. The noisy airboat was not in service, so the advertised offshore tours had been canceled, but the Super Gator Airboat Swamp Tour is not too far away in Orange. I turned around at the impasse and retraced my steps to Big Earl's for a piece of fried chicken. On the way inside, I noticed the

boudin stand across the street where several locals were standing around speaking Cajun French. Here was proof of my original coastal thesis.

Although I had vowed to stay away from cities, I ventured into Port Arthur looking for evidence of Janis Joplin and Robert Rauschenberg, its two most famous natives. At the Museum of the Gulf Coast, where I discovered them both, I watched a movie about the natural and historical development of the coast, learning that millennia ago the broad Gulf stretched all the way to Canada, filling the Mississippi River basin from the Appalachians to the foothills of the Rockies. Exhibits such as "Jurassic to Janis Joplin" and "Buccaneers to the Big Bopper" are illustrated with artifacts, the 1905 Sabine Pass lighthouse lens, for example. The Rauschenberg room was not a history of Rauschenberg's Port Arthur life (he graduated from high school there in 1943), but an exhibition of a few of his smaller paintings. The museum's bizarre collection of decorative arts gathered by Port Arthur residents on travels to far-flung places like Taiwan, Japan, France, England, and Austria is a veritable antique shop. I followed the driving-tour brochure to make one great find — the Eddingston Court gates and wall, fashioned entirely out of 6,000 huge conch shells imported from the Cayman Islands in 1929.

I took the long cut around the McFaddin National Wildlife Refuge (one of many such nature sanctuaries on the coast) to High Island, where about 500 people live on a productive salt dome 45 feet above sea level, amid rusty oil and

gas storage tanks and bobbing pumps. Rich petroleum deposits were first discovered at High Island in 1916, but more recently it has become a famous bird-watching site promoted by the Houston Audubon Society. Like Sabine Pass, it seemed pretty weathered and worn.

Heading down the Bolivar Peninsula, I passed one dead armadillo, some poky-looking cows grazing in hot open fields, and a few more oil pumps. Bolivar is 27 miles long and between one-quarter and three-and-a-quarter miles wide. At the narrow spots, the flat treeless landscape is open to views of both East Bay and the Gulf of Mexico. Scattered stilt houses began to straggle along until they merged into developments with names such as Sand Castles, Copacabana, Holiday Beach, and Noisy Waves. Crystal Beach, about halfway to Port Bolivar, is practically a city, with an AARP Center and Library, a volunteer fire department, and a hospital complex among touristy bathing suit and beach ball boutiques. Passing Rancho Carribe and Kona Kai, I finally reached Port Bolivar, a fishing and cattle center. Like Galveston, its big sister across the bay, Port Bolivar is a substantial town, not just a tourist resort. Most of the 3,500 full-time residents commute to Galveston or Beaumont–Port Arthur; the rest catch and sell seafood or raise cattle and farm.

The highway department has constructed a complex system of traffic lanes leading to the Bolivar ferry landing, but they were empty, so I was happy to find instant passage. During the 20-minute boat ride most people stayed in their cars. I ventured up a narrow staircase to the top deck of the bow, where sailboats,

shrimpers, and huge oil tankers could be seen passing at the end of the day. It was hard not to notice the sandy, sun-burned young lovers in skimpy bathing suits standing next to me, obviously returning from a lazy day at the beach. On the Galveston side, cars were lined up for over a mile to take the ferry home after work.

Galveston is the most famous Texas coast city, and good guides are available, particularly Ellen Beasley and Stephen Fox's *Galveston Architecture Guidebook* (Rice University Press, 1996). The town is a mix of vacationers and old Texas families, world-class late-19th-century architecture and tourist traps. The island evolved gracefully and had a promising economic future until September 1900, when a hurricane caused what is still remembered as the most deadly natural disaster in the history of the United States.

The whole coast of Texas has fallen prey, at one time or another, to fierce weather, and residents are ever mindful of the Great Storm of 1900. Warning systems today should prevent such loss of life; evacuation routes away from the coast are well marked from Sabine Pass to Boca Chica. But catastrophic property loss, not to mention constant salt corrosion and beach erosion, is an ever-present threat. The battered and rusty appearance of much of the coast is not necessarily the result of neglect; it happens when you take a long nap. The hurricane season coincides with summer vacation, giving thrill-seekers the possibility for surfer-scale waves and wild wind with dramatic lightning and thunder. But those who live on the coast are not amused. The eco-

Quintana Beach. Photo by Barrie Scardino, 1997

Port Aransas. Photo by Barrie Scardino, 1997

nomic reality of coastal living is always a catch-up game.

Communities around Galveston and Trinity bays are generally filled with refineries and neighborhoods for those who work in them. There are a few towns that still thrive on sport and commercial fishing. Kemah and Seabrook are such places, with seafood vendors and funky hangouts on the docks. Along Bay Ridge Road at Morgan's Point is a vestige of one of the few summer colonies built on the coast by wealthy Texans at the turn of the 20th century. Several of the large Victorian-era houses are extant, including the wood-frame, gingerbread-clad R. D. Gribble House (1894); the D. E. Kennedy House (1896), with corner towers and a centered turret; and the rambling J. T. Scott House (ca. 1900), with a full complement of screen porches and dormer windows. The Ross Sterling House (1924–27), designed by Alfred C. Finn as an imitation of the White House, is the grandest summer house built on the Texas coast.

Past Lake Jackson and Clute ("Home of the Great Texas Mosquito Festival"), an old two-lane, high arching bridge leads to Surfside — the site of Velasco, the first landfall for Stephen F. Austin's colonists in 1821. Velasco was destroyed completely by a hurricane in 1875. Stilted beach houses, including the requisite Bucky Fuller geodesic dome — of which there was an example in every beach community I investigated — are built up for views and breezes, but more importantly, as a precaution against rising waters, which is sometimes futile. A little farther south, an unsafe-looking old drawbridge leads to Quintana Beach,

where I drove right up onto the sand, which is often possible up and down the Texas coast. I left my car to wander in the waves and enjoy the day's end, but a radio-blaring pickup came barreling down the beach. So much for a moment of peace.

Freeport, just across the Brazos River, is distinguished only by better roads and petrochemical plants. The nearby town of Jones Creek is more satisfying. There I encountered the first of the moss-draped live oaks that give this mid section of the coast, as far south as Rockport, the aura of the Old South along the Atlantic coast. Now dotted with wildlife refuges, this part of the coast was first occupied by large cotton plantations, many owned by families who had migrated from the Southeast.

The intriguing Peach Point Wildlife Management Area portal leads onto a small road that runs beside a magical oak forest. At the head of the road, Peach Point was locked up tight, but directly across was the entrance to Arco's Seaway Jones Creek Tank Farm. I drove past no trespassing signs to find a huge secluded area with more large round oil tanks than I could count. Feeling like a spy, I took a lot of undercover photographs to document this horrific intrusion across from Peach Point.

Peach Point was the plantation of Stephen F. Austin's sister and brother-in-law from 1832, and Austin considered it his home. When he died in 1836, his body was returned to Peach Point and was buried nearby. I have since learned that Peach Point Management Area, with all those fake birds atop its entrance sign, is not a wildlife refuge but a

hunting preserve.

Palacios, at the head of Matagorda Bay, is famous for the Luther Hotel, built as the Palacios Hotel in 1905 with the "longest front porch in Texas." When the Luthers bought it in 1936, they spent five years on a renovation that included remodeling the porch and adding plumbing. Today, standard rooms with a view are $70 to $75 per night including peace and quiet, but not phones, faxes, or TVs. The Luther is a remnant of the simple seaside resort of another time. Landscaped grounds, porch rockers, and a fishing pier provide the only entertainment. Don't come here to rent jet skis.

The fishing and vacation grounds of the Coastal Bend begin in Port Lavaca ("cow port"), which rose on the site of Linnville, a town that disappeared after a Comanche raid that swept down from the Hill Country in 1840. Nearby is the site of another lost town — Indianola, a seaport that once rivaled Galveston. Wiped out by hurricanes and high seas in 1875 and 1887, Indianola is now a ghost town with only its legends and old cemetery.

On the way to Rockport via Highway 35, the preferred coastal route in these parts, I stopped in Tivoli (Tye-VOH-lee) anticipating a greasy lunch at Marie's, which had closed. Tivoli, like Sabine Pass, is not thriving. Rockport, on the other hand, is a mecca for snowbirds, who retire in substantial subdivisions with big lawns and brick houses (not on stilts). Rockport is therefore able to support an arts center, specialty shops, and other city-type amenities. But its two best sights are a 1,000-year-old live oak tree and the Fulton Mansion. The Big Oak

hasn't grown since it was calibrated in 1966 at 44 feet tall and 35 feet in circumference, with a crown diameter of 89 feet. The 30-room George Fulton House was built during the years 1874 to 1876 in the Second Empire style favored by wealthy American Victorians. The Texas Parks and Wildlife Department has restored the house, and it is now a museum open to the public. Like the tree, it is well worth a visit.

In a hurry to reach Port Aransas, I drove fast along the flat coastal plain to Aransas Pass. The ferry, exactly like the Bolivar ferry, provides a short ride to Port Aransas on the north tip of Mustang Island. Ferries and bridges are noteworthy coastal phenomena. The most impressive bridge I encountered was the new Baytown–Goose Creek Bridge; the oldest and ricketiest led to Quintana Beach; and the longest was the Queen Isabella Causeway between Port Isabel and South Padre Island. Bridges and ferryboats provide an important emotional space between leaving and arriving. The sounds and smells of the sea rush through open car windows more urgently on a causeway or ferry, heightening anticipation.

Leaving the Aransas ferry, my excitement about getting to the lighthouse made the refineries and docks I was beginning to accept as part of the Texas coastline seem less intrusive. The privately owned Aransas Pass lighthouse is where I have seen a triple rainbow after a truly frightening storm; it's where I have caught and grilled my supper; it's where I've made good friends; and it's where I find unmatched peacefulness and beauty. From the porch of one of the three houses connected by pierlike catwalks over the marsh flat, I saw vivid roseate spoonbills and split-tail swallows this trip. There are always seagulls, pelicans, egrets, and great blue herons. These birds can be found up and down the coast, but this is where I find them. Historic lighthouses also dot the Texas coast, but I know this one.

David L. Cipra's recent book, *Lighthouses, Lightships, and the Gulf of Mexico*, is a treasury of old photographs and history that pays homage to these powerful forms, which like grain elevators have been rendered almost useless except for their ability to elegantly punctuate a flat landscape. The 50-foot-tall, red-brick Aransas Pass lighthouse tower was constructed in 1855. After a major shift in the Lydia Ann Channel, the lighthouse was decommissioned in 1952. The 1919 keepers' cottage, once a duplex for the keeper and his assistant, is a mottled stucco and frame building that needs constant attention.

Port Aransas, like other Texas coastal towns, has no frills, no glitz. It does have the 1895 Tarpon Inn and the newer Tortuga Flats, where you can come by boat to enjoy the salty crowd and margaritas. The townsfolk prefer Beulah's, a less touristy, but expensive, small restaurant. For those willing to participate, St. Joseph's Island across the Lydia Ann Chanel has a nude beach. Playful dolphin are a common site, as is the Sargasso gulfweed — huge clumps of floating micro-life-infested seaweed that harbors critical food-chain-climbing plants and animals.

Culturally, Port Aransas is not as unsophisticated as it might look — just very accepting. Artists, writers, and other productive nonconformists gravitate here as they do to seacoast villages all over the world. The University of Texas Marine Science Institute employs scientists who study Texas coastal ecosystems, adding another element to the local fishing and industrial population.

Reluctantly leaving Port Aransas, I headed for North Padre Island. Field after field had been bulldozed to make way for new development stretching out south of Corpus Christi. One large cornfield with a "coming soon" sign had been sold even before the corn was harvested. North Padre was not too impressive: there are a few high-rise condos and a lot of people camped on the beach.

To get to South Padre Island, the more celebrated and populated end of this long, sandy barrier island, requires a circuitous route through Kingsville, which is not on the coast, but it is the headquarters of the King Ranch (of chicken casserole fame). On down Highway 77, the only place you can see the water until you reach Port Mansfield is at Riviera Beach, where, after a long drive on a dusty road, I found a bait camp, a boat yard, and the King's Inn restaurant. The big dining room was decorated not with stuffed fish on the walls (did you know that trophy fish are

really painted wooden replicas with only the bill or fin of the real fish?), but with a crystal chandelier hung from the center of the low acoustical-tile ceiling. The fried shrimp and special avocado salad were great.

Backtracking to 77, I saw my first javelina road kill, and blooming cacti were everywhere. Along this 60-mile desert stretch there is no access to the coast. First the King Ranch and then the Kenedy, Armstrong, and Yturria ranches cover Kenedy County, so private land lines the coast along most of the Laguna Madre, which separates Padre Island from the Texas mainland. This part of the drive was boring and hot, but it authenticated scenes from the movie *Giant*.

After Raymondville, where you turn off for Port Mansfield, the desert visibly gives way to the fertile Lower Rio Grande Valley. Fields of high cotton, corn, sugarcane, and acres of soybeans, looking ripe and lush, lined the highways. I arrived in Port Mansfield (which I have heard referred to as "Convict City," presumably because parolees have settled there) the last weekend in July to witness at least one big Texas fishing tournament.

The Port Mansfield Fishing Tournament was headquartered in an empty seafood warehouse filled for the weekend with stalls selling beer and souvenirs, along with weigh stations and finalist boards. Outside, bleachers were set up on the dock for spectators. Every time a boat came in, a couple of TV cameramen and folks who didn't mind the beating sun rushed over to assess the dead fish.

A fancy inboard with a mom, dad, and two boys pulled up, and I hurried over with the rest to see what they had caught. The bright-eyed oldest boy, about 11, with his baseball cap on backwards and a terribly dirty T-shirt, jumped up on the dock to heft the 45-pound cobia, passed up from his father on the boat deck below. Hardly able to carry the huge fish, he rushed it in to be weighed and measured. In a short few minutes he returned to the dock shouting at the top of his lungs, "Dad, we got it!" Having no idea what I was cheering for, I broke into whooping and yelling approval with the rest of the crowd.

As less fortunate fishermen came in, I wandered inside the dark, therefore cooler, warehouse. The nice lady selling T-shirts was from Nebraska, which she and her fish-loving husband had left to settle permanently in Port Mansfield. She gushed with enthusiasm over her adopted community and urged me to consider retiring there too. She didn't look like a convict, and neither did most of the tournament-going families. Seeing flat-bottom boats that glide the smooth shallows of the Laguna Madre in every driveway and an almost-European cluster of party-wall houses bunched up on the bay — old, weathered, and clearly not put up by one developer — I thought I might consider

her suggestion.

On the outskirts of Port Isabel, I found the best photo op since Port Arthur's conch-shell wall — a giant, grand, and grimy octopus lounging on the top of a building. The owner of Sea Caverns Souvenir Shop said the concrete octopus was constructed in the 1950s above an open-porch dance hall. Does the Society for the Preservation of Commercial Archaeology know about this?

I checked in the old Port Isabel Yacht Club (1926), which is now a hotel, after a long day of driving and cheering for fish. This quirky but civilized place had no screaming children, a good restaurant, and a lot of atmosphere in the Spanish-style building overlooking a private marina where respectably sized sailboats cast mast shadows from the setting sun. A small swimming pool surrounded with overgrown tropical plants was cool and deserted, plus it had a side door to the bar where the bartender was happy to put double margaritas in plastic glasses. Why would anyone venture across the bridge to the crowded condos of South Padre? For $45 I had a glorious night's rest in a room with one of those old window air conditioners with no thermostat that hummed sweetly all night as it produced freezing cold air.

Up early, I loaded my courage and camera to assault South Padre Island, where I knew crowds would be filling the moderately priced hotels and motels stretched out along the fine beach. The place was hopping, new construction everywhere. Three flags hung in front of most serious places: Texas, U.S., and Mexico — a nice touch I hadn't seen before. Venturing along the road lined with tourist places to eat, stay, and spend money, nothing very interesting or surprising appeared until, pretty far up the island, I saw what looked like architecture.

The South Padre Island Convention Center has Barraganesque walls of splendid color and complicated glass and steel-frame awnings that jut out and up like the prow of a ship. To the south of the main building, a windowless 300-seat conference theater is covered on the exterior by a fanciful mural of underwater sea life titled *The Whaling Wall*. It was painted by the Hawaiian artist known only as Wyland. The Seattle architectural firm responsible for the San Diego Convention Center — Loschky, Marquardt & Nesholm — designed the complex, which opened in 1992.

A culture and perhaps a century away from Padre Island, Boca Chica is the southernmost point of the Texas Coast. At the "little mouth" of the Rio Grande, it is reached only by Highway 4, a long, narrow road that passes refineries and offshore-rig construction sites much like the ones in Sabine Pass, then scattered houses, trailer parks, fuchsia bougainvilleas, and banana trees, until it becomes an open

lonely road flanked by nothing but marsh, mesquite, cactus, and yucca. A few historical markers along the way tell tales of Civil War skirmishes and young men lost to the elements and disease while waiting in marshy hideouts to fight. The road finally runs right into the Gulf of Mexico across a beach lined with old cars and campers. A rusty red van selling suspicious-looking tacos was the only commerce I saw. The water is muddy and considerably warmer than the water off South Padre Island, due no doubt to the silt and sludge of the Rio Grande emptying into the Gulf down the way.

Turning right at the only intersection near the coast, I found a 1950s-looking three-street neighborhood. The flat houses were dry and dusty like the land, and many of them were empty or boarded up. One man was fixing a car in his front yard, and a few others were out doing nothing. It was pretty deserted. At the very end of the last two-block-long dirt street was a carefully constructed and maintained grotto sheltering a Madonna. She looked over the little neighborhood, not the water. This shrine was the only sweetness or softness I found in Boca Chica, where life is clearly dangerous and hard.

There are no roads over the dunes that separate the main road from the Rio Grande. But there are occasional paths. Venturing up one, I came to the river, which I was shocked to find isn't *grande* at all. It is no wider that a two-lane highway; Mexico is literally a stone's throw away. Over the next dune, I found a fisherman who spoke a little English; I asked if this was actually the Rio Grande. Without smiling he said yes and went back to his fishing. At my third and last lookout, the river seemed even narrower, and I noticed white plastic bags snagged on trees at the river's edge in Mexico. Then I noticed the same thing on my side. They had been tied there to shine in the dark, marking a safe crossing point. I decided it was time to go home. I had come to the end of my journey at a point where the coast is split by nature and politics, where the edge of Texas represents both a barrier and a new beginning. ■

Bolivar Peninsula. Photo by Barrie Scardino, 1997

Port Isabel. Photo by Barrie Scardino, 1997

Mobil Refinery, Baytown. Photo © 1997 Hester + Hardaway

THE ARCHITECTURE OF OIL

Marta Galicki

The oil industry has reconfigured the Texas landscape with wells, pumps, gas stations, refineries, and storage tanks, all of which have made a profound impact on the environment. Corporate towers, research centers, and outstanding residential architecture have been commissioned by companies and families whose wealth was founded on or amplified by oil. The oil elite has also used its wealth to support Texas philanthropies and cultural and educational institutions to an astounding degree. Housing for oil workers and their families began with tents and temporary shacks or simple wooden cottages and evolved into tract housing and residential communities planned and developed by the oil companies themselves. The architecture of Texas towns and cities during this century to a large degree has been shaped by oil money.

Significantly, the modern petroleum industry evolved in Texas as the camera came into common use. Professional and amateur photographers recorded all aspects of the business but particularly the dramatic images of exploration and production. Frank Trost (Port Arthur), F. J. Schleuter (Houston), Charles Steele (San Antonio), Meador (Mexia),

Stephenson and Herkimer (Wichita Falls), and Jack Nolan (Kilgore) among many others contributed to the rich visual record of Texas oil. Walter Rundell, Jr., in his book *Early Texas Oil* (College Station: Texas A&M Press, 1977), presents over 325 historic pictures from the 1860s through the 1930s that provide an intimate view of life in the oilfield as well as dynamic shots of the Texas landscape as it was covered with derricks, pipelines, machinery, and boom towns. The unease and fascination with which modern eyes view these photographs result from the environmental havoc that eventually transpired.

The Texas oil saga began at Spindletop, just south of Beaumont, when Captain Anthony F. Lucas struck one of the greatest gushers of all time on January 10, 1901. By that evening, trainloads of passengers began to arrive in Beaumont. The 500 to 600 oil companies that were set up as a result of Spindletop included the J. M. Guffey Oil Company (Gulf Oil); the Magnolia Petroleum Company (Mobil Oil); the Sun Oil Company (Sunoco); and the Texas Company (Texaco). Officials of the Shell Oil Company from London paid a visit to Beaumont. W. B. Sharp and Howard

R. Hughes's tool company had its origins at Spindletop, as did other oil-related industries. By 1916 Spindletop was almost depleted, but it got a new life in 1925 when the Beaumont wildcatter M. Frank Yount introduced deep drilling techniques. This second boom lasted until 1933 and was concurrent with huge oil discoveries in North Texas and the Panhandle in the teens and twenties in such places as Burkburnett and Borger, in the Permian Basin of West Texas in the twenties, and in East Texas during the Depression, where Kilgore had the densest concentration of oil derricks in the world.

Today at Spindletop, there is not a hint of a hill or any other indication of the Lucas well site. Sulphur mining in the postwar period by the Texas Gulf Sulphur Company caused the land to subside. Tourists are directed a mile away to a pink, granite obelisk dedicated in 1941 to Spindletop and the Lucas gusher. Displaced from its original site, this monument now stands, on a parcel of flat grass adjacent to a freeway interchange outside the recreated Gladys City Boom Town Museum, a frontier theme park. The Texas Energy Museum that was to have been adjacent to Gladys City is

Kilgore, 1943. Photo by John Vachon, courtesy: Library of Congress

housed in downtown Beaumont. The replicated Gladys City is educational but too tasteful and neat. There is little indication of the struggle or exhaustion of oil field work or of its danger, damage, and drama — no working wells nearby, no noises or smells. Gladys City appears sterile and sanitized compared to what period photographs and written accounts suggest that it was: busy, gritty, noisy, muddy, filthy, chaotic, hazardous, and lawless.

Spindletop left Beaumont with a doubled population, enormous wealth, and an oil economy that grew as refineries and pipelines were constructed to accommodate new fields discovered nearby. As a result, successful wildcatters built splendid houses there. The huge Colonial revival house at 1906 McFaddin Avenue in Beaumont was occupied by William P. H. McFaddin, a member of a prominent, old-monied family that increased its wealth when the Spindletop field was brought in on pastureland under its control. Frank Yount's three Beaumont partners, Talbott F. Rothwell, J. H. Phelan, and J. Cooke Wilson, built grand houses in the late 1920s and 1930s, paid for by the recuperation of Spindletop.

Port Arthur, on the western shore of Sabine Lake, was platted by the Kansas City entrepreneur Arthur Stilwell as a seaport and tourist resort in 1895, before the discovery at Spindletop. It was oil that determined Port Arthur's future. John W. ("Bet-a-Million") Gates, the Wall Street investor, became the town's chief financial backer in the early 1900s. His widow, Dellora R. Gates, endowed the Gates Memorial Library in his memory. Located in the town center, this solid neoclassical building was designed in 1918 by Warren & Wetmore, best known for New York's Grand Central Station. Also in Port Arthur, the wonderfully idiosyncratic Eddingston Court, defined by shell-encrusted walls and entry piers [see page 42 this issue], is a private-place development of 1929. It was built for oil tycoons who required the discreet privacy of its charming brick apartments, executed in the Tudor style.

Meanwhile, there was a concerted and successful effort by the financial powers in Houston to lure the oil industry. Soon oil began to compete with cotton as the most important export shipped from the Houston Ship Channel. The industrial development of the channel's waterfront was a direct result of the discovery of oil: the long, protected channel provided an ideal location for oil refineries.

Westmoreland was Houston's first planned elite neighborhood and its first example of the St. Louis-type private place. From 1902 until about 1910, Westmoreland was brimming with oil families: a larger concentration lived there than in any other Houston neighborhood. As soon as the discovery at Spindletop was known, oilman Joseph S. Cullinan moved his operations from Corsicana to Beaumont, and he started the Texas Company there in 1902. By 1905 Cullinan moved his headquarters to Houston, an event considered critical in the establishment of Houston as the oil hub of the Southwest. Cullinan was instrumental in persuading the city of Houston to retain the distinguished St. Louis architect and city planner George E. Kessler to lay out Main Boulevard and plan Hermann Park. He also commissioned Kessler in 1916 to plan the elegant enclave neighborhood Shadyside and invited his oil business associates and friends to build there. Three co-founders of the Humble Oil and Refining Company — R. Lee Blaffer, Harry C. Wiess, and William Stamps Farish — built their houses in the country-house tradition in Shadyside, which features the work of the prominent New York architect Harrie T.

Lindeberg as well as such local architects as Birdsall P. Briscoe, Alfred C. Finn, and John Staub.

But what of the oil workers and their families? The 50-mile Houston Ship Channel transformed the agricultural economy of eastern Harris County into the densest concentration of petrochemical industries in the world. Miles and miles of oil refineries and storage tanks define the industrial towns that line both sides of the Ship Channel with romantic names like Magnolia Park, Pasadena, Galena Park, Deer Park, Baytown, Goose Creek, and Channelview. These settlements are working-class subdivisions that grew out of the agricultural market towns of the late 19th century into early-20th-century petro-suburbs. This was their good fortune and their tragedy. Together they make up the largest area of blue-collar communities in Houston. On the southern shore of the channel, between Deer Park and La Porte, the San Jacinto Monument rises in concert with the refineries.

Magnolia Park in the East End is Houston's most historic Latino neighborhoods. Mexican-Americans started to settle there around 1911 in the wake of the Mexican Revolution. Many early resi-

Burkburnett, 1919. Photo by Herkimer, courtesy: Houston Metropolitan Research Center, Houston Public Library

Housing at the Phillips refinery, Borger, 1942. Photo by John Vachon, courtesy: Library of Congress

dents of this community worked on the dredging and widening of the Ship Channel and later became refinery employees. An active community supporting Mexican cultural and religious institutions evolved. Although Our Lady of Guadalupe parish was founded in 1912, the existing Romanesque brick church on Navigation Boulevard dates from 1923. Still an important landmark in the community, it was designed by the San Antonio architect Leo M. J. Dielmann. In 1935 money was raised in the community to acquire a small piece of land on Buffalo Bayou near the turning basin for the creation of Hidalgo Park. The park was donated to the city, and the Mexican-American community sponsored a spectacular molded concrete kiosk, designed and fabricated by Vidal Lozano.

Pasadena, the largest and best known of the cities along the Houston Ship Channel, is an example of a town that made a shift from an agricultural to an industrial economy in the early decades of this century. J. S. Cullinan's move to Houston required a waterfront site with extensive acreage for Texaco's refinery. He chose a site opposite Pasadena at Galena Park (originally called Clinton). The initial refinery there was constructed by the

Galena Signal Company of Texas, and in 1935 Clinton changed its name to Galena Park.

Deer Park, east of Pasadena on the southern shore of the Ship Channel, was laid out in 1893 by Simeon Henry West.[1] He planted pear trees and chose the name Deer Park because of the abundant deer in the area. The Great Storm of 1900 and the oil discovery at Spindletop three months later meant that his plans for an agrarian community were literally swept away. In 1928 Shell Oil arrived to build a refinery. A tent city, including a school, was established for construction workers and their families. By 1929 Shell was busy building the first suburban housing developments: the Shell City Addition and the Deer Park Addition. These were laid out in a linear suburban pattern and set the tone for subsequent development in Deer Park. In 1940 Humble built a toluene plant in Deer Park for the production of TNT.

Because of the war effort, industry along the Houston Ship Channel increased dramatically. By 1942, 14 refineries plus associated petro-related industries were located along the channel. In 1948 Diamond Shamrock, like Shell, built a plant on the site of "old" Deer

Park, and others soon followed. Deer Park today is a tidy suburban town with open green spaces, shade trees, postwar tract housing, and a hint of prosperity. In the background, separated from the town by the La Porte Freeway, the massive Shell refinery glistens in the sun next to the Ship Channel.

Back in downtown Houston, corporate oil office buildings were under construction. Many of the first generation of oil skyscrapers survive including the Texas Company Building (Warren & Wetmore, 1915); the Humble Building (Clinton & Russell, 1921); the Petroleum Building (Alfred C. Bossom, 1924–27); and the Gulf Building (Alfred C. Finn, Kenneth Franzheim, and J. E. R. Carpenter, 1929). The Tenneco Building (Skidmore, Owings & Merrill, 1963) is still considered a modern classic. One Shell Plaza (SOM and Wilson, Morris, Crain & Anderson, 1971) was the first downtown project of Gerald D. Hines Interests and celebrated the move of Shell's headquarters to Houston. Twin-towered Pennzoil Place (Johnson/ Burgee Architects and S. I. Morris Associates, 1976) is Houston's most significant example of late-20th-century skyscraper architecture.

In contrast to the glassy corporate oil

towers downtown, some companies chose to move to the suburbs. Schlumberger was the pioneer when it built a suburban headquarters (McKie & Kamrath, 1953) along the new Gulf Freeway, which was completed in 1952. The inventive Conoco Headquarters (Kevin Roche, John Dinkeloo & Associates, 1985) is a low-rise, 16-building campus on a 62-acre site in Dairy Ashford. It was built along a stretch of I-10 in West Houston that came to be called the Energy Corridor in the early 1980s because of the concentration of energy corporate offices there.

The ubiquitous gas station is more closely tied to corporate identity than any other product of the oil industry. It began with a need for easily accessible, safe distribution of gasoline. By the 1920s, oil companies were selling a wide range of petroleum products at roadside service stations, and companies like Shell and Humble had begun a nationwide chain of service stations whose the attendants wore standard uniforms. Cleanliness and equal treatment of customers were the order of the day. The earliest generation of corporate gas stations included urban models. In 1918–19 Alfred C. Finn designed Humble's first service station on Main Street and Magnolia's two-story

Humble Oil & Refinery Service Station, Houston. courtesy: Houston Metropolitan Research Center, Houston Public Library

Petroleum Building, Houston. courtesy: Houston Metropolitan Research Center, Houston Public Library

garage-type station on Fannin Street (both now demolished). In Houston, a 1920s service station designed by John F. Staub for the Humble Oil & Refining Company survives as a used-car dealership on Washington Avenue at Henderson Street.

One of Humble Oil's most important acquisitions was its 1938 purchase of the West Ranch, located 22 miles south of Houston on Clear Lake. Humble developed two oilfields there, but ultimately this transaction proved more important for the effect it had on the development of Houston. In 1958 Humble's board gave 22 acres of the tract, along with the large Mediterranean-style ranch house, to Rice University. After Congress began to fund space exploration in the late 1950s, Texas Senator Lyndon B. Johnson was elected chairman of the Senate Aeronautics and Space Committee, and Congressman Albert Thomas of Houston chaired the Independent Offices Subcommittee of the House Ways and Means Committee, which handled the NASA budget. Thomas was also a close friend of several Humble board members. Between 1958 and 1960 Johnson and Thomas "applied heavy political pressure to secure the space headquarters for Houston."[2]

Shortly after John F. Kennedy and Lyndon B. Johnson's inauguration, Humble gave a total of 1,600 additional acres of the West Ranch to Rice, with the understanding that the land be transferred to the United States government for the Manned Spacecraft Center (MSC). By September 1961 it was announced that Houston met all the criteria for the MSC site, and NASA began plans to develop part of the former West Ranch as the MSC.

In 1962 the Del E. Webb Corporation and Humble formed the Friendswood Development Company to develop the remaining 15,000 acres of the West Ranch as a planned new town, Clear Lake City. Humble developed the portion of the ranch fronting Galveston Bay as the Bayport Industrial District. By the 1970s Friendswood had begun to develop Kingwood, a 14,000-acre planned residential community in northeastern Harris County in partnership with the King Ranch. Clear Lake City established a precedent for oil corporations investing in large-scale suburban real estate as can be seen in the Woodlands, a project of the Mitchell Energy & Development Company.

Texas oil families proved to be generous and inspired philanthropists. In Houston, three women had an enormous impact on the direction of architecture and design — Ima Hogg, Nina J. Cullinan, and Dominique Schlumberger de Menil.

In the 1920s, Miss Hogg with her brothers Will and Mike used their personal wealth to finance the development of River Oaks as a model of planned commercial development. Ima Hogg's house, Bayou Bend, was likewise conceived as a model of stylish domesticity. She carried this idea to its logical conclusion by transforming her house and gardens into a showcase of American decorative art, which was opened to the public in 1965 as part of the Museum of Fine Arts, Houston.

In the 1950s Nina Cullinan funded the building of Cullinan Hall at the Museum of Fine arts, designed by Ludwig Mies van der Rohe. Among other philanthropy, Miss Cullinan willed $4 million to the Houston Parks Board.

Dominique and John de Menil commissioned Philip Johnson to design their house and the University of St. Thomas. Howard Barnstone and Eugene Aubry designed the Rothko Chapel for the de Menils, and in 1980 Mrs. de Menil commissioned Renzo Piano to design The Menil Collection in collaboration with the English engineers Ove Arup & Associates. The Cy Twombly Collection, also designed by Piano, was completed in 1995 and her Byzantine Fresco Chapel by François de Menil in 1997.

The economy and culture of oil is materially represented in every aspect of Texas life — corporate towers, elite neighborhoods, refinery towns, cultural institutions, universities, and planned suburbs. Even NASA's destiny was shaped by Texas oil. Although the history of oil tells us that it is a massive generator of wealth, there have been environmental costs that have yet to be fully confronted. ■

1. Patrick Peters, "Deer Park," unpublished manuscript, 1990.

2. Bennett H. Wall and Gerlad Carpenter. *Growth in a Changing Environment: A History of Standard Oil of New Jersey* (New York: Exxon Corporation, 1988), p. 155.

The Toxic Tour of Texas journeys through a state that prides itself on being the biggest, the best. And it is. Texas has the largest concentration of oil refineries and chemical plants in the nation. Texas ranks first in the United States in the amount of known or suspected carcinogens released into the environment. Texas also leads the nation in the number of hazardous waste disposal sites, 70 percent of which leak and threaten ground water. And Texas industry discharges the highest level of toxic air emissions in the country.

The guides on this tour are farmers, priests, mothers, ranchers, engineers, nurses, and teachers who are intent on protecting their land, their children, their homes, and their communities from exposure to hazardous waste. Their activism crosses social, economic, and racial boundaries. This coalition for the nineties aligns the century's labor, civil rights, women's, peace, and ecology movements.

Their united plea is now for the basic life-sustaining elements of clean land, air, and water. They have influenced and reversed government decisions. They have halted harmful industrial practices. They have changed their personal lifestyles, habits, and attitudes as a model of shared responsibility for maintaining this balance of life on Earth.

TOXIC   TOUR   OF   TEXAS

Sharon Stewart

Editor's note: In 1988, writer Steven Fenberg asked photographer Sharon Stewart to attend a legislative strategy meeting of statewide grassroots environmental organizations. After engaging several groups to tell their stories, Fenberg and Stewart set out across Texas to interview these activists, as well as industry representatives and state agencies, in an effort to understand the complex issue of hazardous waste creation and disposal. In 1992 Stewart published Toxic Tour of Texas, *from which she has selected photographs and written updated narratives for this issue of* Cite.

The above introduction to the narrative photoessay *Toxic Tour of Texas* was written with statistics compiled from the Environmental Protection Agency's 1990 Toxic Release Inventory (TRI). When I called the Texas Natural Resource Conservation Commission, the state's licensing and regulatory agency for government and industry air, water, and ground emissions, for the most recent TRI figures (1995), I was disappointed to find Texas still leads the nation in these designations, though overall volume of emissions has declined.

We are a society accustomed to the consumption of convenience and the convenience of consumption. Texas provides a majority of the resources and means consigned to our national defense and enabled us to achieve a standard of living envied all over the world. The issue of creating a balance of resource extraction and maintenance is one of the most contentious in our free-market economy. The driving question of this issue is profitability from present consumptive demand versus sustainability for future supply. Representatives of these opposing forces demonize one another while the consumer citizen looks to the democratic system for protection when something goes awry.

Economics drive this issue. The influence of money, in the desire for profits or influence, continues to be the greatest deterrent to long-term solutions at the legislative, corporate, and personal levels. Our ability to assess the consequences of our consumptive lifestyles is overwhelmed by a cascade of conflicting data from investigative reports, academic studies, congressional findings, lawsuits, and advertising campaigns.

The Tour focuses on Texas citizens who are directly affected by hazardous waste creation and disposal practices and who made the conscious decision to challenge the status quo. The following excerpts from the 1992 Toxic Tour of Texas can make for uncomfortable viewing. A daunting dynamic of perception is revealed in this pressingly complex issue.

How then to proceed as participants in the dynamic? As removed as most of us are from the manufacture and disposal of the items we consume, we are nonetheless affected by their byproducts in the form of reduced air, land, and water quality. It must be remembered that this is of universal concern, contrary to a common response that this is just a Texas issue. Thus, we can reflect on our individual contributions to this dilemma, and alter our behavior. We have been directed how to do so for over 25 years now. How we choose to proceed is as varied as those of you who read this: radicalism, persuasion, or denial. ∎

HUDSPETH COUNTY
MANUELA DOMINGUEZ, MARY ALCORN, IRMA AND CHUY DOMINGUEZ ATOP EL DIABLO PLATEAU OVERLOOKING A PROPOSED TEXAS LOW-LEVEL RADIOACTIVE WASTE DISPOSAL SITE.

"Again and again, the echoing question 'Why here?' rang through my ears as I stood atop the Diablo Rim looking into the beautiful West Texas sunset. Clearly, any proud Texan, if they stood there, would be moved to say, 'This is not the proper place; this is unjust.' The splendor of this land and these people should not be risked merely because the time to choose a site is running short or the Authority has already spent millions to qualify this site."

Judge William Moody, 34th District, presiding:
El Paso County v. Texas Low Level Radioactive Waste Authority

"The people who fight this hinder progress. We will lose a lot of little battles. We will win a war. All they can do is prolong the agony for them and us."

Susan Odom, Public Information Officer,
Texas Low Level Radioactive Waste Disposal Authority

THE TEXAS LEGISLATURE ESTABLISHED THE TEXAS LOW LEVEL RADIOACTIVE WASTE DISPOSAL AUTHORITY IN 1983. EIGHT YEARS AND $30 MILLION LATER, DISTRICT JUDGE WILLIAM MOODY RULED THE AUTHORITY HAD FAILED TO MEET ITS OWN SITING CRITERIA FOR SUITABLE DISPOSAL IN FORT HANCOCK. THE TEXAS LEGISLATURE THEN DESIGNATED A 370-SQUARE-MILE AREA IN THE SAME COUNTY, AND DIRECTED THE AUTHORITY TO ESTABLISH ANOTHER SITE FOR THE DISPOSAL OF LOW-LEVEL RADIOACTIVE WASTE FROM POWER PLANTS IN MAINE, VERMONT, AND TEXAS. BUYING THE 16,000-ACRE FASHKIN RANCH, IN TEXAS'S MOST SEISMOLOGICALLY ACTIVE REGION, AND THEN INITIATING THE REQUIRED STUDIES TO DETERMINE ITS SUITABILITY, THE AUTHORITY CONTINUES TO MEET RESISTANCE FROM LOCAL GOVERNMENTS AND CITIZENS OF THE TEXAS-MEXICO BORDER. IN 1997 THE TEXAS LEGISLATURE DENIED THE AUTHORITY $30 MILLION IN CONSTRUCTION FUNDS, BUT DID APPROPRIATE $6 MILLION FOR THE NUMEROUS LEGAL CHALLENGES IT FACES. A CONGRESSIONAL BILL AUTHORIZING AND FUNDING THE COMPACT AGREEMENT BETWEEN TEXAS AND THE TWO NEW ENGLAND STATES, WHOSE WASTE IT NEEDS TO OPERATE PROFITABLY, WAS DEFEATED IN 1995. THE BILL HAS BEEN REINTRODUCED IN THE 1997 SESSION.

"When the Sesquehanna operation was abandoned, there were seven major piles of waste left. One of the piles was completely away from the uranium mill, across the road on this rancher's property. The tailings were dumped back in a mine that is unlined and sits on top of an aquifer. There's a monument on it now."

Forrest Balser, Karnes County rancher

UNDER PROVISIONS OF THE EPA'S URANIUM MILL TAILINGS RECLAMATION ACT, THE TOPSOIL FROM 700 ACRES OF RANCHLAND CONTAMINATED BY THE SESQUEHANNA URANIUM MILLING OPERATION WAS CONSOLIDATED AND CAPPED, CREATING WHAT LOCALS CALL "THE POD." CHEVRON SOLD ITS MILL TAILINGS POND TO RIO GRANDE RESOURCES, WHICH CONTINUED TO RECEIVE MILL TAILINGS, THOUGH NO MINING ACTIVITY OCCURS. REMEDIATION OF THE POND IS UNDER WAY FOR A PROJECTED FALL 1997 CLOSURE DATE. DR. WILLIAM AU, ENVIRONMENTAL TOXICOLOGIST WITH THE UNIVERSITY OF TEXAS MEDICAL BRANCH, CONDUCTED A HEALTH RISK STUDY IN KARNES COUNTY, FINDING ABNORMAL DNA REPAIR RESPONSE IN COUNTY RESIDENTS. THE PRELIMINARY DATA FROM HIS ENVIRONMENTAL SAMPLING STUDY OF AIR, WATER, AND SOIL FOUND ENVIRONMENTAL CONTAMINATION FROM URANIUM MINING AND MILLING ACTIVITY THAT MAY BE A CAUSE OF THE DNA REPAIR RESPONSE ABNORMALITIES AND MAY INCREASE HEALTH RISKS AMONG COUNTY RESIDENTS.

"What we're concerned about is radioactive particles that go up and latch onto a particle of dust, or get into the water from underground. When you drink, eat, or breathe it, a certain kind of energy radiates in the body that nicks this cell, that cell, this cell again, until it is dead, changed, or growing."

Mike Trial, co-chair,
Panna Maria Concerned Citizens

"We contend that we have not damaged anyone, or will we in the future."

Kevin Raabe, Environmental/Safety coordinator, Panna Maria Uranium operations,
Chevron Resources Company

KARNES COUNTY
MONUMENT MARKING ABANDONED URANIUM MILL TAILINGS SITE. ERECTED BY THE TEXAS DEPARTMENT OF HEALTH, BUREAU OF RADIATION CONTROL.

KARNES COUNTY
CHEVRON'S 160-ACRE MILL TAILINGS POND. CONTENTS: SIX MILLION TONS OF RADIOACTIVE WASTE.

SOUTH DALLAS COUNTY
TIQUESHA ROBERSON PLAYING IN HER YARD ABUTTING WASTE MANAGEMENT, INC. MUNICIPAL LANDFILL IN FERRIS, TEXAS.

"Children that grow up in these types of communities don't feel like they have the same right to become lawyers and doctors and stuff like that, as other kids that didn't grow up in these types of communities. . . . They say, 'I grew up with a dump in my backyard, why should I care if my street's cluttered? Nobody cared about me then.' Children need to know people care about them."
Lorrie Coterill

LORRIE COTERILL'S ORGANIZATION, GROUPS ALLIED TO STOP POLLUTION (GASP), SUCCESSFULLY CHALLENGED THE EXPANSION PERMIT FOR THE SOUTH DALLAS COUNTY LANDFILL IN 1991, PROMPTING ITS CLOSURE. IN THE SAME YEAR GASP ASSISTED FERRIS RESIDENTS IN PREVENTING WASTE MANAGEMENT, INC. (WMI) FROM EXPANDING ITS LANDFILL. HOWEVER, WMI REAPPLIED AND IN 1995 RECEIVED AN EXPANDED MUNICIPAL SOLID WASTER DISPOSAL PERMIT FROM THE TEXAS NATURAL RESOURCE CONSERVATION COMMISSION. THE 667-ACRE FACILITY WRAPS AROUND A BLACK NEIGHBORHOOD WHERE TIQUESHA ROBERSON'S GRANDMOTHER LIVED. LIKE MANY OTHER RESIDENTS OF THE AREA, HER GRANDMOTHER WAS GIVEN $120,000 BY WMI TO RELOCATE TWO FAMILY HOMES. LORRIE HAS JOINED FERRIS RESIDENT VICTOR BURNETT TO CREATE ENVIRONMENTAL JUSTICE, AN ORGANIZATION TO FIGHT THE ACKNOWLEDGED PRACTICE OF SITING HAZARDOUS WASTE FACILITIES IN LOW-INCOME, MINORITY NEIGHBORHOODS.

"They had a permit they could pump up to three million gallons of water a day into the Trinity River. At this point they are not pumping because they are not in full operation. But what is happening now is the liner is actually seeping leachate out of the site into Dumpster Lake, which runs to the river. They knocked down some trees and stuff where it runs into the river right there."
Lorrie Coterill

SOUTH DALLAS COUNTY
LANDFILL BORDERING THE TRINITY RIVER.

NUECES COUNTY
FENCE DIVIDING THE AHLRICH FARM AND A CLASS I
HAZARDOUS WASTE FACILITY.

*"You [Texas Ecologists] told us there would be no
pollution: that the clay pits would never leak. Now
you've got pollution and contamination in the ground
water. We are led to believe the water knows where the
boundary is, and it stops right there, and it won't
cross that line."*
Kenneth Ahlrich

*"The purpose of the monitoring wells is to define the
extent of contamination. But to date, the data that
I've got available does not indicate that it breached
the property boundary."*
Bill Jones, Site Manager, Texas Ecologists

EFFORTS BY THE ROBSTOWN AREA CITIZENS
GROUP, PUBLIC RESPONSE OPPOSING TOXIC
ENVIRONMENTAL CONTAMINATION (PROTEC)
PROMPTED TEXAS ECOLOGISTS (TECO) TO CAP
THEIR CLASS I HAZARDOUS WASTE DISPOSAL
CELLS, THUS ALLEVIATING THEIR STENCH. PRO-
TEC'S PARTICIPATION IN TECO'S PERMITTING
PROCESS ALSO RESULTED IN THE COMPANY BEING
ISSUED A FIVE- RATHER THAN A TEN-YEAR EXTEN-
SION. THE COMPANY HAS EXPANDED ITS OPERA-
TIONS BY 60 ACRES AND IS LISTED IN THE
MCALLEN ECONOMIC DEVELOPMENT COR-
PORATION'S LITERATURE AS THE CLOSEST CLASS
I HAZARDOUS WASTE DISPOSAL FACILITY FOR
USE BY THE MAQUILADORA INDUSTRIES LOCATED
IN NEIGHBORING MEXICO. THE LEAKAGE FROM
TECO'S HAZARDOUS WASTE DISPOSAL CELLS
HAS NOW REACHED THE SITE'S PERIMETER
MONITORING WELLS, ACCORDING TO A COM-
PREHENSIVE MONITORING EVALUATION BY TEXAS
WATER COMMISSION INSPECTORS.

WHARTON COUNTY
THE SINK HOLE INN, A TEXAS HONKY TONK NEAR BOLING, TEXAS.

"On the right is a place we call the Sink Hole Inn. One night it was like a giant lake in the road. The earth just opened up in the middle of the highway, and three pickup trucks drove right into it and disappeared. Luckily, the boys were able to swim out, but the trucks were never recovered. That's what we call a collapse, a sink hole."

Evelyn Freund, Past President, Concerned Citizens Against Pollution

CONCERNED CITIZENS AGAINST POLLUTION'S (CCAP) SUCCESSFUL APPEAL TO THE TEXAS WATER COMMISSION RESCINDED THE PERMITS GRANTED A FRENCH COMPANY, UNITED RESOURCE RECOVERY, FOR INJECTING 1,500 DIFFERENT HAZARDOUS WASTE CHEMICALS INTO THE BOLING SALT DOME, THE WORLD'S LARGEST. OWNERSHIP OF THE INJECTION WELL SITE REVERTED TO THE SELLER, AN AREA RESIDENT. IN MARCH 1993, HIS COMPANY, SECURED ENVIRONMENTAL MANAGEMENT, FILED A HAZARDOUS WASTE INJECTION PERMIT APPLICATION WITH THE NEWLY FORMED TEXAS NATURAL RESOURCE CONSERVATION COMMISSION. IN 1997, THE COMMISSION HAS YET TO ISSUE THE PERMIT. MEMBERS OF CCAP ARE CONCERNED THAT THE SINK HOLES, SUCH AS THIS ONE, INDICATE AN UNSTABLE GEOLOGY FOR STORING HAZARDOUS WASTES IN THE BOLING SALT DOME. THE SINK HOLE INN BURNED TO THE GROUND IN APRIL 1990.

"See that little green box sittin' on that building? That's our benzene monitor I pushed to get. The first in the State of Texas. I love that little box. And right by a playground and baseball field! I know the air here is bad. We have 9,000 emission points into the air from local industry. The highest levels of benzene were picked up right here. Benzene causes cancer."
Rita Carlson

GALVESTON COUNTY
TEXAS AIR CONTROL BOARD BENZENE MONITOR, AMOCO OIL EMPLOYEE BASEBALL FIELD.

THE STATE'S NAMESAKE, TEXAS CITY, RECENTLY GAINED "ALL-AMERICAN CITY" STATUS FROM THE NATIONAL CIVIC LEAGUE FOR ITS EFFORTS TO IMPROVE THE QUALITY OF LIFE IN THIS HOME-TOWN OF SEVEN MAJOR OIL REFINERIES. THREE REFINERIES — AMOCO, MARATHON, AND UNION CARBIDE — HAVE JOINED STERLING CHEMICALS IN A GREENBELT PROGRAM TO BUY OUT LOCAL RESIDENTS WHOSE HOMES BORDER THEIR PLANTS. MAYOR CHUCK DOYLE'S TEXAS CITY GOALS 2000 COMPREHENSIVE PLAN PRO-POSES A GREENBELT INITIATIVE AS A PRIORITY FOR IMPROVING THE AREA'S ATTRACTIVENESS. STERLING CHEMICAL FACES LAWSUITS FROM 5,500 RESIDENTS SUING FOR DAMAGES FROM THE PLANT'S ACCIDENTAL AMMONIA RELEASE ON MOTHER'S DAY 1996. PROMPTED BY HER SONS' EMERGING LYMPH GLAND DISORDERS, RITA CARLSON MOVED HER FAMILY FROM THE PERIPH-ERY OF UNION CARBIDE'S PLANT TO RURAL ILL-INOIS. THE BENZENE MONITOR, LIKE RITA, HAS MOVED FROM TEXAS CITY. THE TEXAS AIR CONTROL BOARD USED IT FOR AN EMERGENCY IN NORTH TEXAS, AND HAS NO PLANS TO RETURN IT. WHILE UNDER OPERATION IN TEXAS CITY, THE MONITOR RECORDED DECREASING LEVELS OF BENZENE IN THE AIR.

"What's in these ditches? A company just put in an application to the Texas Water Commission (TWC) to discharge 2.2 million gallons of wastewater a day into an unnamed roadside ditch that leads to Galveston Bay."
Rita Carlson

"The TWC and the U.S. Environmental Protection Agency have to find a balance of environmental and economic factors in the regulatory process."
John Ward, Water Quality Manager,
Texas Water Commission, District 7

"The TWC is charged to prevent pollution. That's what the Clean Water Act says to do. They do not prevent pollution, they permit pollution, taking the notion that it must be balanced with economic development, and I agree with them . . . but, let's add in the true cost, which is a reduced productive environment. It's a tremendous cost, a huge subsidy."
Brian Cain, Resource Contaminant Specialists,
U.S. Fish and Wildlife Service

GALVESTON COUNTY
OUTFALL DRAINAGE DITCH IN TEXAS CITY.

NO TR SP-SSIN

THIS IS THE PROPERTY LINE OF STERLING CHEMICALS,INC. ILLEGAL DRUGS AND SUBSTANCES,ALCOHOLIC BEVERAGES,FIREARMS,WEAPONS,AMMUNITION, EXPLOSIVES AND ANY OTHER HAZARDOUS SUBSTANCES OR ARTICLES ARE STRICTLY PROHIBITED ON THIS OR ANY OF STERLING CHEMICALS,INC. PROPERTY.

STERLING CHEMICALS

GALVESTON COUNTY
ONE OF 140 HOME LOTS BOUGHT BY STERLING CHEMICALS
FOR DEVELOPMENT AS A GREENBELT ADJACENT TO ITS PLANT.

"The buyout was a gradual thing, but in 1990 we defined boundaries, offered to buy lots and homes, or to relocate families and their homes if they wished. We gave equity advances to find new homes, as well as advances on living expenses. Quite frankly, the liabilities of having people living close to the boundaries of the plant, well, we felt it was a better solution all the way around, in addition to the PR aspects of it."
**Jim McPhail, Public Information Officer,
Sterling Chemicals**

"The Greenbelt is a good idea in as much as it puts some distance between the plants and the population. Is that going to be enough in the event of disaster? I think not. It looks nice. It gives a false sense of security. As you drive through this town, you see that the population lives right on top of this industry."
**Sonny Sanders, Secretary-Treasurer,
Oil, Chemical, & Atomic Workers Union,
Local 4-449**

The Farmers and the Dell Plant

Joel Warren Barna

Dell Plant, Austin. Photos © 1997 Hester + Hardaway

Everything is supposed to be different in Austin now that it is the epicenter of the new economy in Texas. In the new economy, the rules are all rewritten. As George Gilder has said that the global economy has been transformed; no longer is it driven by the need to exploit everything rare and scarce; now it is based on silicon, the planet's most abundant mineral, and ideas, which are endlessly renewable.[1] The new economy has its own miraculous rules: technological advancement can now focus on itself to create its own markets, instead of having to accommodate threatening demographic changes and unpleasantly persistent social needs. As Gilder put it at a conference reported on last year in *Wired* magazine: "My children aren't learning Spanish. They're learning C++."[2]

Metropolitan Austin, which in 1990 was losing population and had the highest suburban office-vacancy rate in the country, is now Silicon Gulch, the boomingest boomtown in the state. Austin now has the strongest job market and fastest population growth in Texas. The national press is paying attention because there are so many restaurants per capita and so many new young millionaires running software companies. This new wealth should be transforming the cityscape, should it not? New clients, in the tradition of generations of Texans with more money than sense, should be pushing local architects to come up with zippy new ideas for their houses and workplaces, as they did 15 years ago in Houston and Dallas, right?

So why, driving around the development crescent that follows the partially completed ring roads westward from Interstate 35 north of Austin towards the highland lakes, does one see nothing at all that is actually new? Why do the fastest-growing parts of Austin and its satellites — Pflugerville, Round Rock, Georgetown, Leander — look so much like Schertz, or Pearland, or Plano, or Albuquerque, or suburban Boston? Why

do the development patterns of this information-revolution landscape so closely mimic those established in the 1960s and 1970s?

This is the metropolitan area with the highest concentration of architects in Texas (roughly eight architects per 10,000 residents, as compared with about three per 10,000 in Houston and four per 10,000 in Dallas), and a long tradition in its large and well-known architecture school of trying to uncover and promulgate an indigenous, regional architectural style for everything from downtown office districts to houses. Why, then, outside of a couple of stylish restaurants most notable for their completely nonregionalist character, is there such a lack of architectural ideas?

FROM DOUGHNUTS TO DOLLARS IN ROUND ROCK

Round Rock used to be famous for little more than its doughnuts, amazing yellow confections sold near the town square. Now, what only a few years ago was scraggly farm land right off IH-35 has sprouted the utterly utilitarian looking Dell Computer plant, headquarters of a company that has posted over 1,000 percent gains in revenues and stock value in the past five years, putting Round Rock in the national news every time the company issues one of its quarterly reports. Not far away, two-year-old Power Computing manufactures Macintosh clones in the shell of an abandoned Wal-Mart; it is one of the fastest-growing start-ups in the history of the computer industry. And some of its employees say they have developed a strong taste for those Round Rock doughnuts. A little farther north, in Georgetown, the Del Webb company has opened the first 5,300 acres of Sun City, a thoroughly commonplace looking suburban community (very like the new Sun Cities Del Webb is building near Hilton Head, South Carolina, and Scottsdale, Arizona)

for retirees over 50 that has brought Williamson County its first bocce ball club.

Follow the roads from Round Rock to the swelling suburbs of Hayes County in the south, and you are looking at one continuous pattern. You have your tilt-wall warehouse park beside the freeway, your mirror-glass or limestone midrise office clump and shopping center where the freeway intersects a major thoroughfare, your apartments near the shopping center, and your pod-and-connector-road housing developments spread back into the former cotton fields, away from the high-priced land. The houses are more vertical than they would have been 30 years ago, and more of them are clad in limestone, and they certainly cost a lot more in real terms. But otherwise the pattern is the same as it has been for decades.

Austin, with just enough topographical variation to ease eyes bored by endless horizons, with its spring-fed swimming pools and downtown night clubs and cheap apartments providing memories of youthful indulgence for the hundreds of thousands who attended the University of Texas and went on to their real lives elsewhere, has always been one of the most easily imageable of Texas cities. But now it is being transformed into a placeless place, yet another iteration of America's coast-to-coast Stripville.

THREE CULTURES

The reason for this transformation is that the new Austin is split among three cultures — Corporate World, Slacker Mecca, and the Displaced Atavists — and none of the three requires any particular architectural expressiveness, fitting seamlessly into the prefabricated patterns of postwar American development.

Corporate World is perhaps the least familiar of new Austin's personalities — nobody has made a movie about it to match *Slacker*, and it doesn't have a talk-

radio voice as do the Displaced Atavists. But it has a long and completely unremarkable history, based in the military-industrial complex, with public money seeding private enterprise (just the sort of thing that George Gilder says never works). In the 1960s and 1970s, Tracor and Texas Instruments built plants in Austin to capitalize on the abundance of electrical engineers and other college-trained employees provided by the University of Texas at Austin, and both companies prospered on federal Defense Department contracts. IBM and Motorola joined them, drawn also by the work force, and had become major local employers by the late 1970s, building consumer goods. The Motorola facilities in Austin were the site, in the 1990s, for the creation of the Power PC chip for Macintosh computers. And the IBM Austin plant is where the company developed and manufactures the hot-selling Thinkpad laptops, which were about the only ray of hope for the company a few years ago.

Another big change came in the 1980s. With the Cold War waning, America discovered that its industrial base was threatened by competition, primarily from Japan. Two research consortiums with broad backing in industry and government, Sematech and MCC, were organized to foster technological innovation that would turn the tide. Competing against high-tech centers in California and the East Coast, Austin was chosen for both, because of the presence of the existing companies, the workforce, and the political influence of its congressional delegation. With the example of these efforts, along with Austin's relatively low cost of living, other companies moved to the city, including Advanced Micro Devices (manufacturers of computer chips that compete with those of Intel), Tokyo Electron, and the Korean electronics giant Samsung, which is spending several hundred million dollars on new facilities. And in the midst of this, local boy

CHANGE WITHOUT CHANGE IN AUSTIN

Michael Dell took his IBM-clone-making company from an operation he ran out of his apartment as a UT undergraduate to a multi-billion-dollar company with more than 8,000 Austin-area employees — a number reportedly growing by more than 100 per month for the past year.

Although there has been a lot of migration to Austin, with scores of Californians arriving daily during that state's recent economic recession and attendant floods, earthquakes, and lethal mudslides, it has not been enough to keep up with the demand for high-tech employees. Samsung, with its plant still under construction, has begun working with Austin Community College on training courses for its prospective workforce. Country radio stations run ads for Dell Computer in which good ol' boys discuss leaving their dead-end lives behind to get new jobs at the Dell plant. Radio spots for Advanced Micro Devices feature joggers comparing the perks at AMD with those of other, lesser companies. The real attraction that Californians and others find in Austin, which has been a major factor in the growth of the last decade, is that Austin remains comparatively cheap: housing costs in Silicon Gulch are only about half those in California's Silicon Valley.

The relatively low cost of living is the connection between Corporate World and Slacker Mecca, although many of Austin's musicians and artists find themselves priced out of the neartown neighborhoods by the new high-tech competition. The success of the big hardware manufacturers has created a penumbra of related development. There are now thousands of software developers working in Austin, writing everything from networking software to games, and their presence is more and more visible, particularly in the central city. When the Temple-Inland Mortgage Company left its office building on Congress Avenue for a new office complex southwest of downtown, the downtown space was leased by

Human Code, a drop-dead-hip games developer. Austin's image as a place with a higher-than-average body-piercings-per-capita ratio has been both a cause and an effect of the growth of the software-development industry, particularly those parts devoted to creating games and entertainment. Workers in these companies are much more likely to sport the tattoos and T-shirts that are young Austin's dress code than are their counterparts in the hardware manufacturing companies. Here is where the Slacker ethos not only survives but prospers.

There have been other spin-off effects. The number of advertising and graphic design firms has doubled in the past three years, and more and more of Austin's musicians and recording technicians are finding work serving the high-tech industry's marketing needs. Even architects have benefited: Graeber, Simmons & Cowan has carved a niche in the design and construction of fabrication plants for Motorola, Advanced Micro Devices, and other companies, while RTG Partners has designed most of the new buildings for Dell Computers, as well as the master plan and the major buildings of Sun City in Georgetown.

The biggest urban effect of new development will be from the projects completed and being planned on West Sixth Street and 38th Street. Austin's street pattern provides only one easy connection between downtown and the western suburbs of Tarrytown and West Lake Hills, along Sixth Street. Similarly, only 38th and 45th streets connect the medical center area with the suburban homes of the city's doctors and a sizable number of college professors. This pattern channels most of Austin's prosperous people into a couple of roadways twice a day, and the urban pattern is shifting dramatically in recognition. Sixth Street at Lamar used to be a zone of automobile dealerships and historic houses. Then the Ford dealership moved out to IH-35 and Whole Foods opened an enormous store there, head-

quarters of what was once a little hippie grocery and is now a publicly held nationwide retailer. Austin's largest advertising agency, GSD&M, has a new building next door (designed by RTG Partners) and touts itself as "Idea City." The Chevrolet dealership is moving next, to be replaced by several hundred thousand square feet of retail, office, and entertainment space. A 20-screen movie theater and a Target store are also planned for the area. The 38th Street corridor is seeing growth every bit as dramatic. The state Department of Mental Health and Mental Retardation has been auctioning off empty land from the Austin State Hospital grounds that is being converted for retail buildings, offices, and apartments.

DISPLACED ATAVISTS — THE HEIRS OF CRITICAL REGIONALISM

Listen to talk radio in Austin and it becomes clear that, despite the rapid growth of the new Austin, the city still has a sizable population of men and women with a distinctly rural outlook, only a generation at most from the farm. The folks, already suspicious of UT and the state government (still the largest employers by far), now also see themselves as displaced by the forces of the new Austin — all those Koreans, and the kids with the shaved heads, and the nose rings, all the traffic, the sense that crime is rising, and the cost of living. And to a large extent they have been displaced, both literally and figuratively, as the landscape gets remade, forced to move farther north and east from the city's edges. The result, as one can hear daily, is a state of frustrated, atavistic dudgeon, with constant calls to turn back the clock competing with the news of new plants and housing starts.

It seems doubtful that architecture critic and historian Kenneth Frampton had Austin's Displaced Atavists precisely in mind as he made the rounds of the

Texas architecture conferences in the mid-1980s. Talking up his concept of a "critical regionalism," what Frampton described was the architectural expression of a local resistance to the economic and social power of late capitalism and the emerging globalized economy. It sounded interesting at the time, although one doubts that any such project could have the leftward spin of Frampton's ideas.

Instead, as shown in Austin, critical regionalism, with its ties to the old forms of landscape and building that are nostalgically evoked in contemporary houses, is an inherently conservative idea. The people who try to hold back the globalization of the culture are not the remnants of the 1960s: the transformation of Whole Foods into a national chain shows how that strain has been neutralized. It is the Atavists, who have migrated to the northern fringes of the city, to Pflugerville and Round Rock and Georgetown, who periodically try to stop the tide of change that the high-tech companies bring with them. Thus the Williamson County Commissioners Court was the only voice of protest when Apple Computer wanted tax concessions to open a service center near Round Rock — protesting not Apple's blackmail of local taxpayers but the company's liberal policy on health benefits for domestic partners, including homosexual domestic partners.

Poised between three cultures, none of which has the strength to dominate, the new Austin is a landscape still searching for a characteristic mode. It will be interesting to see, if the economic miracle continues, what emerges over the next decade. ■

1. Po Branson, "George Gilder: Does he really think scarcity is a minor obstacle on the road to techno-Utopia? (And would he please stop talking about race and gender?)," *Wired*, March 1996.
2. Ibid.

A Few Words About

TEXAS MOVIE LANDSCAPES

Jon Schwartz

Brewster McCloud, 1970.

*"Each landscape is formed
by the point of view of the
spectator; it is a spiritual
experience, the reflection
of a culture."*

Magnum Landscape, *1996*

Now a century old, movies are the backward-glancing time machines of our collective and ever-changing landscapes. At best, they give us something memorable to dream and think and expand upon: in *Giant*, James Dean paces off his inheritance, a parched and seemingly worthless strip of land that will soon be wet with oil. At worst, they mix the reel with the real so as to obscure and confuse: in *JFK*, Oliver Stone edits staged Dallas grassy-knoll footage with 22 seconds of Zapruder documentary — 28 years later. Let the viewer beware! These Texas landscapes aren't always what they seem to be. But sometimes they're a lot more.

While post–World War II movies set in New York City or London or Paris were satisfied to capture a local ambiance, Texas-based movies required mythic landscapes to complement their more-often-than-not mythic narratives. Chronologically, these evolved as historical myth, stories set in the 19th century that pitted man against a hostile landscape; family saga myth, stories set in the 20th century wherein the landscape has been harnessed, freeing the generations to clash among themselves; and cartoon myth, a last-gasp lampooning of our Texas myths.

Red River (1948) is Howard Hawks's mythic retelling of the first cattle drive to Abilene. In the film's early scenes, an extended montage chronicles John Wayne's trek across Texas: crossing the Red River south through the Panhandle and past the Pecos, finally finding good cattle range near the Rio Grande. It matters not that none of these "Texas" landscapes are actually Texas. The logistical problem of moving 1,500 head of cattle from location to location forced Hawks to shoot the entire film in Arizona. And though the Arizona mountains seem too big, at least Hawks gives us lots of Texas-like big skies and wide-open spaces.

John Ford's *The Searchers* (1956) begins with "Texas, 1868" superimposed on a black screen. A cabin door opens revealing a color landscape that looks nothing like Texas and in fact is unmistakably Monument Valley, director Ford's favorite location. Ford poetically places John Wayne's stoic searcher of the title amid the majestic rock formations of Monument Valley in an epic quest to find his niece, taken captive by Comanches. Would this film have been as visually mythic had Ford filmed in Texas? Probably not. In short, it's not very good Texas — but it's great John Ford.

John Wayne's *The Alamo* (1960) mixes authenticity with Hollywood artistic license. Reproduced to scale, the Alamo mission displayed the humped gable and upper two windows not present at the time of the 1836 battle. The film's secondary set, San Antonio, 1836, was strictly a Hollywood concoction. As Frank Thompson writes in *Alamo Movies*, "San Antonio looks very little like a Mexican town of the period, which were constructed around a series

of plazas; *The Alamo*'s San Antonio looks like a conventional western town."[1] Perhaps this was a concession to James "Happy" Shahan, owner of the 22,000-acre Brackettville ranch where *The Alamo* was filmed, who — when Wayne's financing dried up — found monies to complete what became known as Alamo Village. In the long run, this generic Western set turned out to be of more value than a period Mexican town; Shahan has since brought over 30 productions and thousands of tourists to Brackettville.

Filmed in Marfa, George Stevens's *Giant* (1956) is an epic for its 201-minute running time alone. Bringing his Virginia bride home to Reata, a sprawling cattle ranch, Rock Hudson and Elizabeth Taylor ride for miles in a convertible over a roadless desert. At first a speck on the horizon, a three-story, seven-gabled house comes into view. Out of place in the desert, this Gothic edifice provides a unique setting for this saga that covers 25 years of changing traditions and shifting social orders.

In 1963, Martin Ritt brought Larry McMurtry's *Horseman, Pass By* to the screen as *Hud*. Ruthless son Paul Newman and principled patriarch Melvyn Douglas clash over turning their cattle range into oil leases. Douglas: "What can I do with a bunch of rotten oil wells? . . . I can't breed 'em or tend 'em or rope 'em." Newman: "There's money in it." A 19th-century cattleman to the end, Douglas says, "You can get the oil after I'm under there with it." A 20th-century man without tradition, Newman rides not a horse but a pink Caddy through the film's black-and-white Panhandle landscape. Of this landscape, McMurtry has written: "The camera was completely faithful to the beauty and pitilessness of the Panhandle. It showed what is there, a land so powerful that it is all but impossible to live on it pleasantly."[2]

If *Brewster McCloud* (1970) is any indication, Robert Altman wasn't enamored of the Texas landscape — nor did he buy the Astrodome's Eighth-Wonder-of-the-World hype. An image of Houston's smoggy downtown skyline gives way to bird crap splattering on a *Houston Chronicle* front page lining a bird cage, and this is just the opening credits. One scene has bird-woman Sally Kellerman bathing nude in the Mecom Fountain— no longer a mere fountain but revisualized as a Texas-size birdbath. In the film's main plot (such as it is), title character Bud Cort wants to fly in the Astrodome. Like Icarus, who flies too close to the sun and falls to earth, so too Brewster flies too high in the Dome and falls to his death. Altman's message is clear: The Astrodome can be hazardous to your health.

Steven Spielberg's *The Sugarland Express* (1974) is a live-action cartoon, with Goldie Hawn as the Road Runner mom wanting to retrieve the baby taken from her, and Ben Johnson as the Wile E. Coyote highway patrolman who unwit-

tingly leads a procession of more than 200 cars — police, media, curiosity seekers — in hot pursuit. Spielberg's landscape is one of cars and roads: stolen cars, highway patrol cars, cars with gun racks, used-car lots, car wrecking yards, highway road markers, gas stations, police roadblocks, and lots of car crashes. Obviously, this was before "Drive Friendly" signs dotted the Texas landscape.

Once a genre has been lampooned, can the revisionists be far behind? The quintessential small-town Texas movie is Peter Bogdanovich's *The Last Picture Show* (1971), which co-screenwriter Larry McMurtry calls "a kind of anti-*Giant*."[3] "Anarene, Texas, 1951. Nothing much has changed," reads the film's poster. The film ends as it begins, with a slow pan of the town's main street. It all looks the same, except now the picture show has played its last movie (appropriately *Red River*). Ironically, nothing much has changed — and yet everything has changed. Small-town America has died.

And so it is with these landscapes. Nothing has changed, and everything has changed. Frame by frame, *Giant* is the same movie in 1997 that it was in 1956. In 1956, scenes of cattle grazing amid oil derricks might have seemed ironic, whereas in 1997 they are, as McMurtry has suggested, "an elegy not merely for the cattlemen but for the wildcatters too."[4] In 1974, The *Sugarland Express* procession might have seemed Capraesque. Today, in light of O.J., the same landscape seems definitely more somber.

It's a short 23 years from the montage of cowboys yahooing the cattle in *Red River* to Chill Wills yahooing the guests down the corridor of the Shamrock-like hotel in *Giant,* and back full circle to the scene of cowboys yahooing the cattle in *Red River* that flickers the Royal Theater to a close in *The Last Picture Show*. In 1997, as I gaze at the landscape with the shuttered movie theater that fills Bogdanovich's last frames, I'm suddenly aware that something else besides small-town America has died. Perhaps movies as an art form have also died. Little did I realize in 1971 that the poetry of post–World War II cinema would soon give way to the cacophony of theme-park-ride cinema. I wonder what I'll see in this landscape when I rescreen *The Last Picture Show* in another quarter century. ■

1. Frank Thompson, *Alamo Movies* (East Berlin, Pa: Old Mill Books, 1991), p. 73.

2. Larry McMurtry, "Here's HUD in Your Eye," *In a Narrow Grave* (Albuquerque: University of New Mexico Press, 1968), p. 17.

3. Larry McMurtry, "Men Swaggered, Women Warred, Oil Flowed," *New York Times*, Sept. 29, 1996, p. H15.

4. Ibid.

A TEXAS MOVIE LANDSCAPE THAT MIGHT HAVE BEEN

If *The Last Picture Show* is the quintessential small-town Texas movie, what then would be its urban equivalent? Unfortunately, there is none. But had Billy Lee Brammer's *The Gay Place* (Austin: Texas Monthly Press, 1978) ever been filmed, things might have been different.

Set in an unnamed place resembling Austin, Brammer's book is comprised of three novellas linked together by a common landscape presided over by a Lyndon Johnsonesque governor named Fenstemaker. Upon its 1961 publication, *The Gay Place* (its title taken from an obscure F. Scott Fitzgerald poem) found few readers in spite of considerable critical acclaim: Brammer was likened to Fitzgerald, and his novel was hailed by the likes of Gore Vidal and David Halberstam as being the best ever written about American politics.

It didn't take long for Hollywood liberals Paul Newman and director Martin Ritt to become interested. The husband-and-wife writing team of Irving Ravetch and Harriet Frank, Jr. was hired to pen the script. With a talent for writing colloquial dialogue, they had previously adapted two Faulkner titles (*The Long Hot Summer* and *The Sound and the Fury*) as well as Texas writer William Humphrey's *Home From the Hill*. Ritt, Newman, and Ravetch/Frank later collaborated on *Hud*.

However, the movie was never made. In a letter to the author, Larry McMurtry recalled: "I remember being in Austin when Martin Ritt tried to make *The Gay Place* from a script by the Ravetches. That was in 1962. Rumor has it Lyndon Johnson had it squelched with a few calls."

It's our loss that a great, visionary filmmaker never made the film: Orson Welles, who had tangled with William Randolph Hearst over *Citizen Kane*, might not have been so easily intimidated by LBJ. Or, given the novel's multi-character narratives, Robert Altman might have made a companion film to stand alongside *Nashville*.

"Billy Lee Brammer's death at 48 in 1978," writes William Broyles in his forward to *The Gay Place*, "extinguished a sensibility and talent that could have just possibly made Texas a universal landscape as the London of Dickens or the Spain of Hemingway." As readers, we can be grateful for the one landscape he did write, complete with State Capitol, Governor's Mansion, college tower, caucus rooms, beer gardens, and even a desert film shoot. (Brammer had visited Marfa during the filming of *Giant*).

And perhaps a Welles or an Altman might have been equally inspired, giving us memorable movie landscapes to rival the Gothic house in *Giant* or Anarene's Main Street in *The Last Picture Show*. Will a good movie ever be made from *The Gay Place*? Probably not. Unless of course Harrison Ford can be cast as Fenstemaker. *J.S.*

McMURTRY'S HOUSTON

Sims McCutchan

Others have written about Houston, but none more intimately than Larry McMurtry. Five of his novels are set, at least in part, in Houston and several of his essays also include observations about the city. *Moving On* (1970), *All My Friends Are Going to Be Strangers* (1972), and *Terms of Endearment* (1975) belong to Houston of 30 years ago: before the boom and the bust of the 1980's, before today's impressive skyline, and before the influx of newcomers altered the city's demography. *Some Can Whistle* (1989) and *The Evening Star* (1992) return to a much transformed place, a fact McMurtry does not fail to note.

In the Houston novels, the city transcends mere setting and becomes a character itself — unmistakably female. Danny Deck, the narrator of *All My Friends Are Going to Be Strangers*, reflects: "Houston . . . had been my mistress, but after a thousand nights together, just the two of us, we were calling it off. It was a warm, moist, mushy, smelly night, the way her best nights were. The things others hated about her were the things I loved: her heat, her dampness, her sumpy smells."

McMurtry's affair with this swampy demoiselle began during his undergraduate period at Rice (1954–55) and was rekindled when he returned as a graduate student (1958–60), living just off campus in a garage apartment at 1718 1/2 Rice Boulevard. Later as a member of the Rice English faculty (1963–72), he lived at 2219 Quenby in Southampton, where, as recorded by Tom Wolfe in *The Electric Kool-Aid Acid Test*, Ken Kesey and his bus full of merry pranksters first touched down in Houston. The Rice neighborhood figures prominently in McMurtry's portrait of Houston, but the writer's eye for local color roves considerably to River Oaks, the Heights, the East End, and Denver Harbor. The names of actual streets, bars, restaurants, and shopping centers frequently appear undisguised; even when altered and amplified to fit the demands of storytelling, the places themselves are still usually identifiable.

McMurtry favors inner city neighborhoods to suburbs, although his first collection of essays, *In A Narrow Grave* (1968), came close to being titled *The Cowboy in the Suburb*, because "[it was] essentially that movement, from country to subdivision, homeplace to metropolis, that gives life in present-day Texas its passion. Or if not its passion, its strong, peculiar mixture of passions, part spurious and part genuine, part ridiculous and part tragic." His bias was expressed by one of his most memorable characters, the Boston-born-and-bred widow Aurora Greenway, who was "opposed to the whole concept of suburbs, though it appeared that suburbs were where most people lived . . . In her youth . . . there were towns, villages and country . . . none of this muddle of stoplights, convenience stores and small ugly houses in between."

Aurora's inventor is particularly adept at describing aspects of Houston the Chamber of Commerce would rather forget. In the 1968 essay, "A Handful of Roses," he writes, "If one were to choose a single aspect of Houston, and from that infer or characterize the city, I would choose its bars." Some of the most vivid and hilarious scenes in the Houston novels occur in blue collar bars and honky tonks catering to east Texas hillbillies come-to-town, called "citibillies" by McMurtry. They favored places like the New Frolic, J-Bar Korral, Tired-Out Lounge, and Breaking Point Lounge: "seldom fancy but reliably dim and cool . . . equipped with jukeboxes, shuffleboards, jars of pig's feet and talkative drunks." Telephone Road, teeming with ice houses and beer joints, is the location of Gulf Air Lounge, featured in *Moving On*. Here a customer expresses his disapproval of a bean-deficient bowl of chili with a barrage of gunfire. At present, the few remaining bars on Telephone Road are either Korean cocktail lounges or Latino cantinas, but the glory days of redneck watering holes remain preserved in McMurtry's picaresque prose.

In "A Handful of Roses," McMurtry observes, "one can view the most extraordinary example of Mexican saloon and whorehouse architecture north of the border" on McCarty Drive. He may have had in mind a place called Harbor Lights, a large honky tonk frequented by stevedores, truck drivers, and sailors. It is tamer now — a "sports bar." McCarty Drive was also the location of J-Bar Korral, a dance hall where Royce Dunlap, husband of Aurora's maid Rosie, drives his potato chip delivery truck through a flimsy plywood wall and onto the dance floor in a fit of jealousy. Not far away on Clinton Drive is the Athens Bar and Grill, the presumptive model for the Acropolis, which Aurora Greenway visits in *The Evening Star*. Other East side venues make appearances in *Terms of Endearment*. Royce and Rosie Dunlap live in Denver Harbor on Lyons Avenue. At one point, Rosie seeks employment as a car-

hop at a drive-in on Lyons (Pioneer Drive-In No. 16), and, for a while, Royce cohabits with a waitress girlfriend in a tiny apartment on Harrisburg next to "a mountain of some 20,000 worn-out tires."

In *Some Can Whistle*, Danny Deck's daughter works at a place called Mr. Burger on Dismuke Street near Lawndale Avenue. Returning from Los Angeles in search of her, Deck first wanders into Houston Heights, where he stops for a meal at a taco stand on Twentieth Street. McMurtry owned an antiquarian book store, Booked-Up, at 711 Studewood in the Heights during the 1980s.

Not far from the Heights on Washington Avenue, Aurora samples the culinary delights of the Pig Stand No. 7, a coffee shop and erstwhile drive-in specializing in pork sandwiches, fried onion rings (which it claims to have invented), and other delicacies not on the American Heart Association's recommended diet. In *The Evening Star*, Aurora's old friend and former suitor General Hector Scott quietly dies at the Pig Stand after sampling "a bite or two of her mince pie." The movie was filmed on location with waitresses filling in as extras; booth 6 is now commemorated with a plaque as "Aurora's booth." The Pig Stand also features a collection of more than 2,000 miniature pigs.

Rice University and its surrounding neighborhoods appear in all five Houston novels. In *Moving On*, Rice graduate student Jim Carpenter and his wife Patsy live in a garage apartment behind a South Boulevard mansion. His fellow student and friend Flap Horton lives with his wife Emma in similar quarters on less fashionable West Main in Montrose. In *All My Friends Are Going To Be Strangers* Danny Deck has memorable encounters with a disapproving librarian at Fondren Library. Some of McMurtry's most lyrical passages about Houston are conveyed through Deck as he walks through the campus and its environs.

In *Moving On*, the Hortons and the Carpenters join other graduate students at a Mexican restaurant on Almeda Road, which closely resembles Spanish Village, an affordable, Christmas-tree-light illuminated shrine of classic Tex-Mex food and unwatered margaritas. The group sits on a covered, open-air porch at heavy, chipped-tile-top concrete tables. Today the porch is enclosed and air conditioned, but the tables remain just as McMurtry described them.

Aurora and her friend, Trevor, visit The Last Concert, a "small Mexican

bar . . . on an obscure street in North Houston." They dance the samba, cha cha, and rumba in this "after hours" refuge until six in the morning. Three decades later, The Last Concert plays on at 1403 Nance Street in the Warehouse District on the northern edge of downtown, and its patrons are still obliged to knock on the door, speakeasy style, for admission.

Danny Deck pays a visit to the Angel Bar on Elysian Street just north of downtown in *All My Friends Are Going To Be Strangers*. The bar's neighborhood is not a place for the faint hearted. "Loud jukeboxes blared in the bars. Loud talk rang on street corners. Many knives were carried. At night guns went off and women were pounced on." In a "Handful of Roses," McMurtry, discussing Houston bars, laments that: "my own sentimental favorite, the Angel Bar on Elysian Street, is now alas defunct; and I have never been able to find out if it went broke or all the patrons killed themselves off."

"Love, Death and the Astrodome" was written in 1965 when the dome's charms were thought to be semi-eternal. Rereading this essay in light of recent developments, one appreciates all the more McMurtry's deflationary wonderment at the spectacle of "the huge white dome poked soothingly above the summer heat haze like the working end of a gigantic roll-on deodorant." Exiting the dome after seven lifeless innings between the Astros and the Mets, McMurtry reflects: "Though it is a very pleasant place to watch a sports event, it is much more the product of a love of money and ostentation than of a love of sport. It caters quite successfully to what is least imaginative in the national character."

As for the character of the city itself, McMurtry had higher hopes. Despite its past and present as an "opportunist's delight," he speculated in "A Handful of Roses" that there was yet the chance that Houston might mend her ways and acquire a modicum of respectability: "She may, with her money and her sexy trees, attract the sort of imagination that could bring her to a rich maturity and make her a mother city. Even now she is being fecundated by a diversity of peoples, and her children might be interesting to know. They will be natural urbanites, most of them, members of the first generation of Texans to belong in fact and in spirit to a fertile city, not to the Old Man of the country or the Old Maid of the town." ■

The Texas Room, Houston Metropolitan Reserarch Center, Houston Public Library. Photo © 1997 Hester + Hardaway

THE TEXAS ROOM

Stephen Fox

The Texas Room, as everyone calls the Texas and Local History component of the Houston Public Library's Houston Metropolitan Research Center, is my home away from home in downtown Houston. It is located on the second floor of the Houston Public Library's Julia Ideson Building, in what was the principal reading room of the Central Library Building from 1926 until 1975.

It's a tall rectangular room, lit by arched windows along both sides that admit views of the downtown skyline, the greenery in front of City Hall, and a big pink parking garage. Even when the vibrations of passing trucks shake the floor and sirens pierce its calm, the Texas Room remains an oasis of tranquillity. It's where I escape the grinding sensation of downtown sidewalks. Perhaps it's the cool putty-gray color that the walls are painted and the way they contrast with the white plaster decoration, the bright red carpet, and the lustrous oak furniture.

When Eugene Aubry and Sally Walsh designed the restoration of the Julia Ideson Building 20 years ago, they compensated for the overcrowding that the building had endured before construction of the present central library in 1975 by emphasizing spaciousness and quiet. Amazingly, despite two decades of subsequent growth and the incorporation of new technologies, the Texas Room preserves Aubry and Walsh's arrangements: long parallel rows of library tables and chairs, which were installed in the building when it opened in 1926; the vista from what was once the delivery hall, separated from the Texas Room by a transparent glass partition; even the vista through the closed stacks to a distant window facing Smith Street and the green reflections on the Allied/First Interstate/ Wells Fargo tower.

The open volume — an unwitting spatial pun — establishes the Texas Room as a place of clarity and calm, an imaginative space where researchers can embark on long journeys through place and time. But the Texas Room is not only a place of escape, it's a place of engagement and discovery. It's where I go to track down historical information on communities and buildings throughout Texas that I can't easily visit.

My Texas Room bible is the *Texas General Contractors Association Monthly Bulletin*. It lists buildings in the process of being designed by architects and construc-

tion contracts awarded, and it covered the entire state from 1922 to 1937. The Texas Room possesses the only copies known to exist. What its original subscribers considered a throwaway is now a resource of statewide significance.

The Texas Room also has lists in many different forms. My favorites are the old city directories and telephone directories from throughout the state. A close second is the collection of hundreds of maps and photographs, old and new. The Sanborn fire insurance maps, published for insurance purposes and updated at intervals, show building outlines for Texas towns beginning in the 1880s. One can trace the spatial evolution of many towns for nearly a century, since the Sanborn Company continued to revise the maps until the early 1970s.

Then there is supporting evidence for the seriously bloody-minded — like newspaper clippings going back to the 1920s, or ad valorem tax rolls for Texas counties from 1836 until, in some cases, the early 20th century. Sounds like a snooze? Not if you're trying to track the date of a building by ascertaining the year that the valuation on its real estate experienced a noticeable increase. You do find yourself

wishing that those who entered the information wrote in a clearer hand with fewer scriptorial flourishes. And why did the microfilmers reproduce handwritten records in such a small format?

U.S. Census schedules are another Texas Room resource. More mind-numbing tedium? Well, yes, but you wonder what motivated an enumerator to categorize a householder as "insane." No matter how perfunctory or bureaucratic the records, you keep stumbling across all these human-interest enigmas that draw you in and make the past seem a lot less remote.

In the Texas Room you can lay hands on the disparate threads that lead to a connection between here-and-now and there-and-then. This search for continuities does not seem critical to the daily lives of most of my contemporaries, which makes the Texas Room even more special to me. It's where I go in the hope of recovering lost truth and forgotten memory. ■

TEXAS BOUNDARIES

Texas Boundaries: Evolution of the State's Counties *by Luke Gournay. College Station: Texas A&M Press, 1995. $29.50.*

Taking Measures Across the American Landscape *by James Corner and Alex S. MacLean. New Haven: Yale University Press, 1996. $40.00.*

Reviewed by Danny Marc Samuels

To make a mark upon the land is a fundamental act of design. Those particular marks that subdivide and measure the surface of the earth into a mosaic of usable or saleable or governable areas occur simultaneously at many scales, from global meridians and latitudes, to national and local political boundaries, to individual property lines. Although themselves conceptual and invisible, these artificial constructs interact with the natural landscape to create the most enduring designs we make.

The intricate overlay and interplay of these sets of lines of survey tell an evolutionary history. Like cracks in mud, the surface is first broken into large areas, and successive cracking events fracture it into ever smaller areas. There is continual accommodation, warpage, and deformation as historical accidents become permanently embedded into the pattern. As property is divided, roads laid down, fences stretched, buildings built, boundaries adjusted, plants grown, the invisible lines become more and more manifest and more permanently etched. Even over centuries, whatever else changes, the demarcation persists.

On the ground, these patterns are perceived almost subliminally. We may not be aware of the particular geometry of the landscape in which we stand, but we sense a profound difference between a rural English landscape with irregular plots formed by the wanderings of cows and separated by hedgerows, and a Midwestern gridded landscape with straight trajectories of roads and wire fences dividing 40-acre rectangles. Viewed from the air, however, the nature of the mosaic and its evolutionary history become apparent. Who cannot gaze for hours from an airplane window upon the ever-fascinating pastiche of land uses laid out before us?

The view from a plane crossing the United States reveals a changing panorama that reflects the unfolding history of the country. The original colonies on the East Coast inherited the patterns of Europe — boundary lines for the most part followed natural features in irregular configurations. Soon the pressure of migration into the western territories necessitated a system for apportioning and selling the land from remote offices. As early as 1785, nine years after the Declaration of Independence, the Continental Congress was concerned about how to demarcate the western territories, and, with the Enlightenment influence of Thomas Jefferson, passed a land ordinance that set forth endless ranges of townships divided into 36 square-mile sections (640 acres). A rigorous and artificial rectangular order was indelibly impressed upon the natural landscape. Over time, Congress encouraged westward settlement by making ever smaller parcels of land available to more people for homesteading, eventually reducing, through successive quarterings, the square mile to the 40-acre family plot. Curiously, the land ordinances provided only for boundary lines; rights-of-way for roads had to be taken from adjoining land. (The story of the U.S. survey was told in detail in Hildegard Binder Johnson's *Order Upon the Land*, 1976, unfortunately long out of print.) Over time, the basic rectangular survey was overlaid by other geometries and scales: the diagonal vectors of the railroads in the 19th century, the crystalline grids of towns that were first oriented to river fronts or railroad lines, then fractured to align with the survey grid and later, in the 20th century, with the sinuous sweeps of interstate highways, which immediately and completely transformed the character of towns and cities. And now, the lines of air routes, telecommunication beams, and Internet connections are even more invisible, but no less landscape-altering.

The dominant characteristic of the Midwestern American landscape has always been orthogonality: gridded farms, gridded towns. The grid has often been criticized for its banality or authoritarian nature. But in fact, as Spiro Kostof points out, the grid has no intrinsic political viewpoint; it is simply a neutral framework within which anything may happen, be it Manhattan, Iowa, Chicago, or Phoenix. It may, indeed, be construed as most democratic, infinitely accommodating and flexible, modified by alteration and overlay, taking on the character of whatever is going on within it, and maturing eventually into a rich complexity. And certainly, in its contrast to nature, with which it coexists, the grid has a compelling beauty of its own.

The land development history of Texas, as a glance at a county map of Texas shows, seems to recapitulate that of the United States: an initial irregular geometry on its east (Gulf) coast is transmuted into a rectangular pattern in the west. The watershed areas along the coast were settled first, mostly by European and American impresarios who enjoyed enormous Spanish land grants beginning in 1821. With Texas independence in 1836, the original 23 eastern counties, roughly based on the land grants, had county seats along rivers, with boundaries surveyed back from and perpendicular to the river. Land was measured in leagues (4,428 acres), 5,000 by 5,000 *varas* (the Spanish unit of measure, later fixed at 33 1/3 inches). After Texas joined the United States in 1845, the original enormous counties were progressively subdivided, and large blocks of new counties were periodically added to the north and west, usually in ranges following orthogonally along latitude lines — 31 new counties in the northeast in 1846, 29 down the center in 1858, 54 in the Panhandle in 1876. A new state constitution in 1876 provided rules for county creation: new counties created from unorganized land could not be smaller than 900 square miles (30 by 30 miles), and they had to be as square as possible; when counties were subdivided, each part had to be at least 700 square miles; and county seats had to be centrally located. Texas was not subject to the U.S. survey system, but land subdivision within counties, because of the influence of the railroads, sometimes followed the mile-square system, although it was discontinuous and often oriented to the rail line rather than to the compass points. By 1921, the present configuration, with 254 counties, was essentially formed. From the point of view of land surveys, Texas is a crazy quilt, with no consistent orientation or measure at all.

Most of *Texas Boundaries: The Evolution of Texas Counties*, a slim, dry history that recounts the process of county formation, is virtually a chronology detailing the origins of every Texas county. Unfortunately, the book is limited by dealing only with county lines, and not other aspects of land survey in Texas. This book's interest, however, lies in its graphic presentation, which consists of a sequence of maps (computer generated by the author) showing the county subdivision at successive points in history, with new counties highlighted. This amounts almost to a freeze-frame animation, which, when regarded in sequence (one imagines flipping the pages), imparts an impression of the actual evolution in time of the map of Texas. As such, this book introduces a new technique into the repertoire of landscape representation.

Another recent book that greatly expands the repertoire is the stunning *Taking Measures Across the American Landscape*. Here Alex MacLean's sumptuous aerial photographs are thoughtfully juxtaposed with map drawings: collages of drawings, paintings, and photographs by landscape architect James Corner. Together they graphically explore a wide sweep of the landscape history of the United States, from the sacred land markings of Native Americans, through panoplies of geometry brought by diverse settlers, to various ramifications and peculiarities of the rectangular survey, to the large-scale effects of modern transportation, agriculture, water, energy, and military projects. There is more than enough thoughtful text (the historical essay by British geographer Denis Cosgrove is particularly enlightening) to provide a firm scholarly grounding to the rich visual mix.

These books indicate that new ways of regarding and representing the landscape can render new insights. A book (or CD-ROM) that combines a rigorous and thorough history with a detailed and engaging graphic presentation, however, has yet to be produced. Perhaps — as in the parable recounted by Jorge Luis Borges and Adolfo B. Casares (*Extraordinary Tales*, 1971) of the obsessive king who commissions the royal cartographers to make a detailed map of the kingdom and ends up with a map at a 1:1 scale, exactly covering the kingdom itself, and no place to put it — we are wishing for too much. ■

During a certain season in Texas, at dusk, some tree trunks seem to be phosphorescent . . . they give off a dull, blazing light. Upon close scrutiny it is found that the trunk of the tree is completely covered with discarded shells that were the outer body of certain insects. The startling fact is that the shell is intact; the form is exactly as it was when its original inhabitant was inside, with one difference. The inside has left, leaving the outer form, which looks like an x-ray, producing the luminous effect. Suddenly we hear a chorus of sound coming from the dark leaves above. It is the sound of the insects hidden in the tree in their new metaphysical form. What is strange about the phenomenon is that we can see the insects' shell forms clinging to the tree, empty shells, a form that life has abandoned. While we fix our eyes on these apparitions, we hear the sound of the insect in its new form hidden in the trees. We can hear it but we cannot see it. In a way, the sound we hear is a soul sound.

John Hejduk

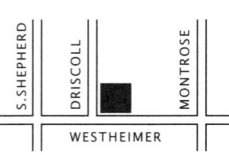

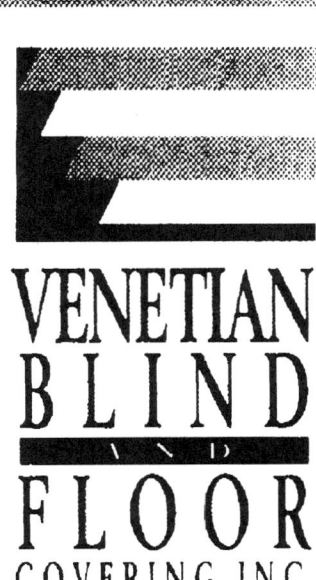

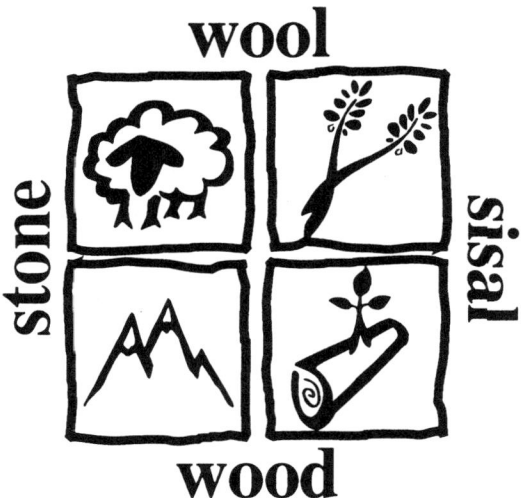

The Powell Group

Design

Space Planning

Computer-Aided Design & Drafting

Furniture Specifications

Finish Selections

Installation

Inventory Evaluation & Management

Installation Documentation

Installation Coordination

Refurbishment & Repair

Warehousing

QUALITY

EXPERIENCE

RELIABILITY

THE POWELL GROUP, INC., SPECIALIZING IN SALES AND SERVICE OF OUTSTANDING FURNITURE FOR THE WORKPLACE.

The Powell Group, Inc. • 5599 San Felipe • Suite 555 • Houston, Tx 77056
Telephone: 713. 629. 5599 • Fax: 713. 629. 4600

R. RICHARDSON LTD.

"THE SWORD CHAIR"

COMMISSIONING AND MAKING FINE FURNITURE

CATALOG AVAILABLE
P.O. BOX 55344, HOUSTON, TEXAS 77255-5344
TEL (713) 547-1711   FAX (713) 236-1245

ligne roset

1800 Post Oak Blvd, Suite 182
HOUSTON, TEXAS 77056
713/629.7722

WE'VE SPENT THE LAST SIX YEARS BUILDING THE HISTORY OF TOMORROW

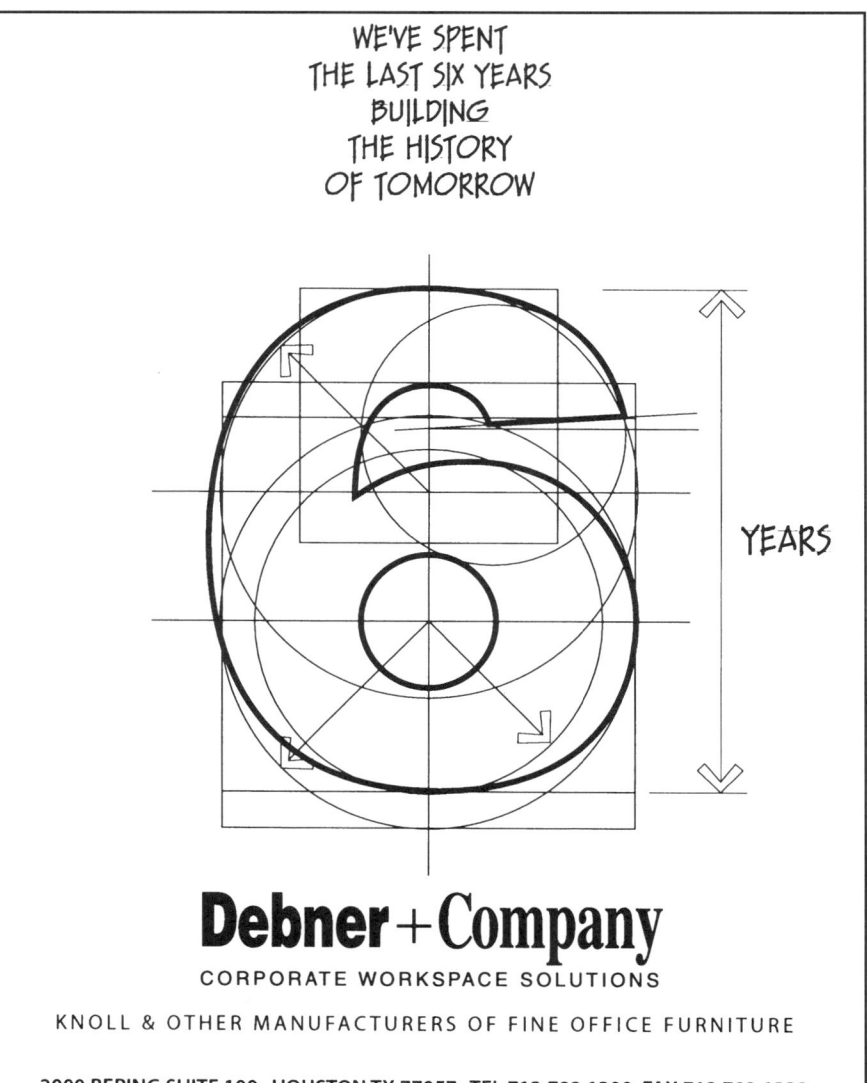

YEARS

Debner + Company

CORPORATE WORKSPACE SOLUTIONS

KNOLL & OTHER MANUFACTURERS OF FINE OFFICE FURNITURE

2000 BERING SUITE 100 HOUSTON TX 77057 TEL 713.782.1300 FAX 713.782.1332
Email: knoll@debner.com

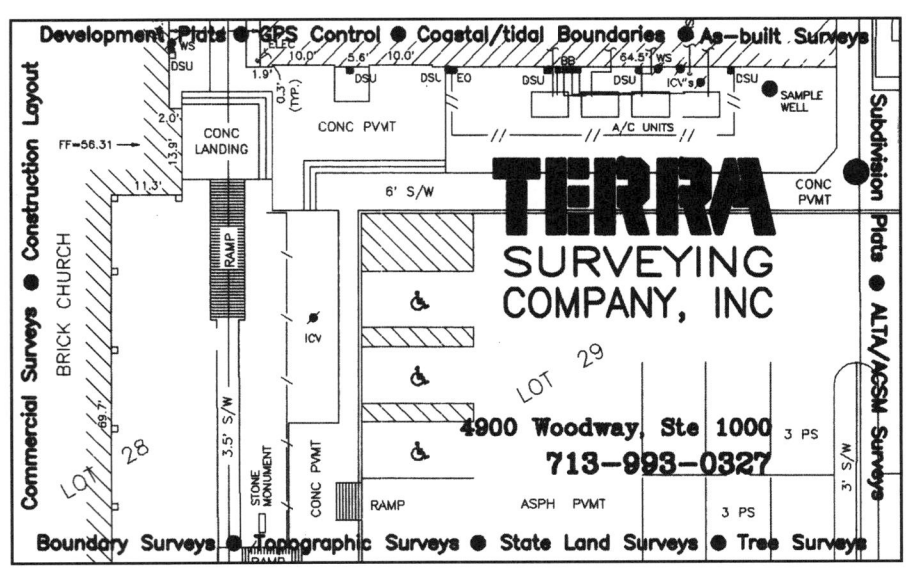
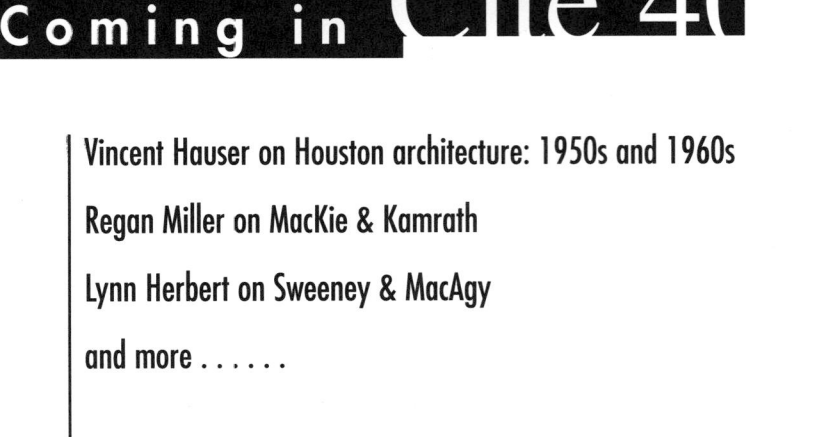

Coming in Cite 40

Vincent Hauser on Houston architecture: 1950s and 1960s

Regan Miller on MacKie & Kamrath

Lynn Herbert on Sweeney & MacAgy

and more . . . . . .

Back cover: Photo by Thomas Colbert

Cite Calendar

A Publication of the Rice Design Alliance

OCTOBER 1 THROUGH OCTOBER 22

RDA Lecture Series:
1900–2000: American Cities in the Twentieth Century
This series will look at four American cities as they have matured over the last 100 years. The lectures will examine dynamic changes that have occurred in American urbanism and their effects on the architecture and physical nature of cities. *Brown Auditorium, MFAH.* 713.527.4876.

OCTOBER 1 — WEDNESDAY — 8:00 P.M.
New York: Kenneth T. Jackson
Professor and chairman of the department of history at Columbia University, editor of *The Encyclopedia of New York*, and author of *Crabgrass Frontier: The suburbanization of the United States*.

OCTOBER 8 — WEDNESDAY — 8:00 P.M.
Chicago: Robert Bruegmann
Professor of art history at the University of Illinois at Chicago and author of *The Architects and the City: Holabird & Roche of Chicago, 1880–1918*.

OCTOBER 15 — WEDNESDAY — 8:00 P.M.
Los Angeles: Kevin Starr
State librarian of California, professor in the school of planning and development at the University of Southern California, and author of *Inventing the Dream: California through the Progressive Era*.

OCTOBER 22 — WEDNESDAY — 8:00 P.M.
Miami: Nicholas N. Patricios
Professor of architecture at the University of Miami and author of *Building Marvelous Miami*.

SEPTEMBER 24 THROUGH NOVEMBER 12

RSA: Cullinan Lectures
Dave Hickey
Associate professor of art criticism and theory at the University of Nevada and author of *Air Guitar: Essays on Art and Democracy*.
"The Deplorable Consequence of Architecture as Drawing" (September 24, 7:30 p.m.) *Brown Auditorium, MFAH.*
"Hong Kong Aesthetics: Post Industrial Architectural Practices" (October 29, 7:30 p.m.) *Farish Gallery, RSA.*
"In the Palace of the People: New Lessons from Las Vegas" (November 12, 7:30 p.m.) *Farish Gallery, RSA.* 713.527.4864.

OCTOBER 5 THROUGH NOVEMBER 2
Film Series:
Cinemarchitecture VII: American Cities
In collaboration with the Rice University Media Center, RDA will sponsor this series to complement its fall lectures: *1900–2000: American Cities in the Twentieth Century*. *Rice Media Center.* 713.527.4853.

OCTOBER 5 — SUNDAY — 7:30 P.M.
New York: *The Empire State Building*
A comprehensive documentary of New York City's timeless monument from its 1920s conception to the present (1995, 55 min).
New York: *Manhattan*
Woody Allen plays a successful television writer struggling through ill-fated romances with a high school senior (Mariel Hemingway) and a schizophrenic (Diane Keaton) who is having an affair with his best friend (1979, 96 min).

OCTOBER 12 — SUNDAY — 7:30 P.M.
Chicago: *The Loop, Where the Skyscrapers Began*
Architectural historian Vincent Scully presents the revolutionary architecture of "the Loop," Chicago's downtown area named for the cable car route later replaced by "el" trains (1992, 30 min).
Chicago: *Medium Cool*
A remarkable semi-documentary about the effects of television on our lives and perceptions. Filmed mostly in Chicago by award-winning cinematographer Haskell Wexler, it focuses on a television news cameraman mechanically going about his life in the midst of the volatile events of 1968 (1969, 110 min).

OCTOBER 26 — SUNDAY — 7:00 P.M.
Los Angeles: *Cadillac Desert*
This story of the American West is about the relentless quest for water. This state-of-the-art exposé focuses on William Mulholland and the controversial projects that brought water to the desert town of L.A. (1996, 90 min).
Los Angeles: *Chinatown*
Jack Nicholson is an L.A. gumshoe involved over his head in an intricate web of murder and political corruption concerning a fortune in land and water rights, led by femme fatale Faye Dunaway (1974, 131 min).

NOVEMBER 2 — SUNDAY — 7:00 PM
Miami: *Resorts — Paradise Reclaimed*
This segment from the series "Pride of Place — Building the American Dream: A Personal View by Robert A. M. Stern" investigates Americans' desire to return to nature — not the untamed nature their pioneer ancestors encountered, but a comfortable and peaceful evocation of a rustic past (1986, 60 min).
Miami: *Some Like It Hot*
Musicians Jack Lemmon and Tony Curtis witness a Chicago gangland massacre and then elude the mobsters by dressing in drag and joining an all-woman band (Marilyn Monroe is the ukulele player) heading for a posh resort hotel in Miami (1959, 120 min).

OCTOBER 8 THROUGH NOVEMBER 19

GHCA Lecture Program
The fall lectures of the Gerald D. Hines College of Architecture, University of Houston will include Olivier Arene and Christine Edeikins (October 8); Jacques Hondelatte (October 15); Imfried Windbichler (October 23); and Charles Gwathmey (November 19). *Architecture Building, UH.* 713.743.2400.

OCTOBER 20 — MONDAY — 6:30 P.M.
GHPA Good Brick Awards
The annual Good Brick Awards ceremony will recognize architectural preservation in the Houston area. Brown Auditorium, MFAH. 713.216.5000.

OCTOBER 25 — SATURDAY — 7:30 P.M.
GHCA Gala: *The Blueprint Ball*
The third annual benefit will honor the 52nd anniversary of the Gerald D. Hines College of Architecture. Proceeds will provide financial assistance to UH architecture students and support for programs that benefit the UH architectural community. Outstanding Alumni Achievement Awards will be presented to Solomon S. Pan, FAIA (Hall of Fame); Donald Meeks, Jr. (design); Brit Perkins (community development); and Robert Atra (architecturally related field). *Architecture Building, UH.* 713.743.2353.

NOVEMBER 14 — FRIDAY — 7:25 PM
RDA Gala: *HI-YO SILVER!*
RDA will celebrate its 25th anniversary at this year's gala with dinner, dancing, and a silent auction. Entertainment will be provided by Ezra Charles & The Works, Commercial Art, and Steve Draper Entertainment. The 1997 Award for Design Excellence will be presented to Anne Schlumberger Bohnn Brown, who has supported architectural scholarship, research, and education in Houston through programs and publications of the Anchorage Foundation of Texas. A special 25-year award will recognize developer and financier Jesse Holman Jones, whose vision shaped downtown Houston. *The Petroleum Club.* 713.527.4876.

NOVEMBER 16 THROUGH FEBRUARY 1

MFAH Exhibition:
The Dark Mirror: Picasso and Photography
The first U.S. exhibition of Pablo Picasso's rare photographic work is organized by the MFAH and the Musée Picasso, Paris. *MFAH.* 713.639.7300.

Deans' Lecture Series:
Houston Talks
RDA, the Rice University School of Architecture, and the Gerald D. Hines College of Architecture, UH will again collaborate on a series of lectures that will occur in the fall and the spring. This collaborative program features international architects who are invited to give public lectures and to spend time with architecture students of both schools. *Speakers and dates to be announced.* 713.527.4876.

FEBRUARY 25 THROUGH MARCH 25

RDA Lecture Series:
Architecture in Furniture and Fashion
Furniture and fashion have been given little critical attention within architectural culture despite their inevitable complicity with architecture as a discipline. Furniture is for rooms, fashion is in the street, and buildings stand in the middle. Draftsmanship, be it manual or virtual, is the craft they all share. They are also equally invested in dimensions of timelessness vs. temporariness, utility vs. excess, structure vs. supplement, not to mention relations of space and the human body. Once unraveled, the architectural implications of furniture and fashion might offer renewed sources of inspiration for the practice of architecture itself, just as they may provide architects with new resources for their design education. *Wednesdays; speakers to be announced. Brown Auditorium, MFAH.* 713.527.4876.

APRIL 25–26 — SAT. AND SUN. — 1–5 P.M.
RDA Architecture Tour:
Houses by Katharine Mott
Katharine Mott began her career in the 1920s designing houses in Indianapolis. She moved to Houston in 1927, bringing her carpenter and brickmason to maintain her high building quality standards. Mott, with Burns & James Architects, eventually designed and built more than 20 houses in River Oaks, Riverside Terrace, Edgemont, and Devonshire Place. Several of these houses will be featured on this annual members-only tour. *Memberships available at the door.* 713.527.4876.

Please call 713.529.2483 to be included in our winter CiteCalendar as space allows. We cannot guarantee that all requests can be included.

Abbreviations:
GHCA: Gerald Hines College of Architecture, University of Houston
GHPA: Greater Houston Preservation Alliance
MFAH: Museum of Fine Arts, Houston
RDA: Rice Design Alliance
RSA: Rice School of Architecture